The Woman's Business Therapist

The Woman's Business Therapist

Eliminate the MindBlocks and RoadBlocks to Success

Marcia Rosen

Chandler House Press
Worcester, Massachusetts

The Woman's Business Therapist:
Eliminate the MindBlocks and RoadBlocks to Success

Copyright © 2000 by Marcia Rosen

ISBN 1-886284-55-5
Library of Congress Catalog Card Number 99-068775
First Edition
ABCDEFGHIJK

Published by
Chandler House Press
335 Chandler Street
Worcester, MA 01602
USA

President
Lawrence J. Abramoff

Director of Publishing
Claire Cousineau

Editorial/Production Manager
James A. Karis II

Book Design and Production
John Woods, CWL Publishing Enterprises

Cover Design
Janet Amorello and Michele Italiano-Perla

Cover Photo
Larry Stein Photography

Chandler House Press books are available at special discounts for bulk purchases. For more information about how to arrange such purchases, please contact Chandler House Press, 335 Chandler Street, Worcester, MA 01602, or call (800) 642-6657, or fax (508) 756-9425, or find us on the World Wide Web at www.chandlerhousepress.com.

Chandler House Press books are distributed to the trade by
National Book Network, Inc.
4720 Boston Way
Lanham, MD 20706
(800) 462-6420

CONTENTS

DEDICATION

This book is dedicated to women!
For all you do!

INTRODUCTION

*T*he *Woman's Business Therapist* draws on my experiences as an entrepreneur for over 30 years. When I opened my first business, women owned only 4% of all small businesses as compared with today's proportion of 50% and more in many major cities across the country. Women want their own businesses for many good reasons: an opportunity to utilize their talents, be their own boss, have flexible hours, control their own lives, enjoy independence, earn a decent living, and make a lot of money.

I began to be called a business therapist because of my method of advising women entrepreneurs about their businesses and my ability to help women business owners move beyond the difficulties that arise time and time again that can keep them from being successful in business. I knew the women entrepreneurs I met were smart, capable, and talented. Yet, most were struggling to "survive and thrive" in their businesses. I found there were very specific issues related to being a women business owner that they really needed to talk about with someone.

What made a difference in my meetings and conversations was when I would ask them, "What's really going on here?" Over and over, I found the question opened the door to both serious and humorous discussions with hundreds of women business owners about the problems they were experiencing.

Many women acknowledged and expressed to me something was missing or amiss. Then I asked more questions. "How are you dealing with the frustrations and challenges?" "How can we work together to help you move past the stumbling blocks that are interfering with your business success?" I listened a lot. I paid attention to their concerns and upsets. And what I discovered, over and over, was that women entrepreneurs face both Mind-Blocks and RoadBlocks to success.

The RoadBlocks are the external obstacles. The business world has been and can be "women unfriendly," where sexism, discrimination, and stereotypes prevail. The National Association of Women Business Owners (NAWBO) has stated, "The greatest challenge of all is being taken seriously, and that includes proving our capability and credibility." The demands on our business and personal lives require a major balancing act. In fact, we all know that for most of the 20th century women have not been trained, encouraged, or given access to business.

We can also be on the hurtful end of some pretty nasty comments when we are very successful. "She's too pushy." "She's a bitch." "She must have a rich husband." "She's ugly." "She probably can't get a man; she's ugly." (That one is said a lot.) We've been conditioned to feel that not being the most adored, lovable creatures on earth is totally unacceptable.

At what enormous cost to us? We don't say aloud how we really feel. We may not even say it clearly to ourselves. We do say it by our actions, by our deeds, by our words, by our body language, by our attitudes, by our holding back, by our lying, by our pretending, by blaming and faking and keeping secrets. Sometimes it seems too difficult and overwhelming to do quite everything we need to do to reach that place we dream of that has long been kept quiet in our hearts and screaming in our souls.

The MindBlocks are those internal issues that need to be treated the same way you would handle personal and relationship problems. Look at the symptoms listed at the beginning of the book. Explore the truths behind the symptoms that are all too often running us. The messages we received as young girls-the expectations of us as we became women, as dictated from generation to generation and relived in each family-have a huge impact on who we are and our decision-making processes.

This book addresses those business, social, personal, family, and historical issues women encounter as they start and grow a business. This book gives you solutions that work and new ways of seeing things so you can be set free to live your dreams and ambitions.

This book is my vision of how to make things better for women, especially women who seek financial security as well as economic independence through success in business.

There are 12 business therapy sessions, as I see them, that examine the major issues that I believe interfere with success and happiness in business. Spend some time on your own Personal Profile and Symptoms analysis at the beginning of the book. Be honest with yourself! What symptoms do you relate to? You'll find you will relate more to some symptoms than to others. Each session will help uncover many of the truths about the symptoms and expose many of the secrets and limitations that prevent you from reaching that place you know you're capable of reaching. Acknowledge your own secrets!

The stories that follow might give you reason to pause. Some of them may sound like you. In fact, they are about women I have counseled and women who have responded to my work, as well as my own experiences. And finally, each session offers proven and practical advice to help you move beyond the limiting mindsets and behaviors. You may want to keep a journal or notebook close by so you can write down your thoughts, feelings, and concerns-perhaps even some of your secrets and wishes. Create an action plan for yourself. Reading this book may move you to want to explore further, to ask for more help from business consultants and therapists, or to attend workshops.

This book is a big step for you to gain the insights into your own stumbling blocks. I encourage you to take the risk to move beyond your own MindBlocks and RoadBlocks.

Mostly, I wrote this book because I want to tell women, "You don't serve the world, your community, your family, or yourself well by being less than what you are capable of being." As accomplished women, we make an impact on ourselves and on others. We become role models and mentors and we have something to offer the world and ourselves well into our 80s and 90s.

Did you know that in 1890 a woman attorney named Belva Lockwood Plain won the right for married women to keep their paychecks? That was just a little more than 100 years ago. While it makes me think we women have come a long way, it also reminds me of the terrible places we've been.

Today, across the U.S. women own more than 50% of all small businesses. There are over eight million women-owned businesses in the U.S., employing over 18.5 million people. Home-based women owned businesses in the U.S. number 3.5 million and provide full- or part-time employment for an estimated 14 million people. Today we generate more than $3 trillion annually in sales. Staggering numbers! We have forever changed the world for women.

Virginia Woolf, in *A Room of One's Own*, articulated women's need for private space. The room is a symbol of independence, dignity, and certainly courage. I feel strongly that every woman needs money of her own. It generates independence and dignity. I know you have a heart. I know you have a brain. I believe you have the courage to surmount even major obstacles and to move beyond the MindBlocks and RoadBlocks that hold you back!

—Marcia Rosen

PERSONAL PROFILE AND SYMPTOMS

Each chapter in this book is designed as a business therapy session. These 12 sessions address primary issues that interfere with business success and happiness for women entrepreneurs. However, for this book to really help you move beyond your interferences, you have to identify your personal symptoms-the distresses, upsets, anxieties, and complaints that cause you to want to throw your arms up in the air and give it all up, scream at anyone in sight, kick the dog, or spend the weekend eating chocolate somethings.

Check off your symptoms. Even if you have only one symptom relating to any given session, please read that session. One symptom can be enough to cause you a lot of grief and heartache and hold you back! The beginning of each session offers insights into the symptoms and into the secrets that keep the symptoms in place. At the end of each session are solutions.

SESSION 1: MONEY

❑ Money is a problem for me.
❑ I don't feel comfortable discussing money.
❑ I'm not good at collecting money due me.
❑ I don't know how to negotiate fees or contracts.
❑ I never know what to charge for my services.
❑ I don't really understand business finance.
❑ I don't have anyone I can trust with whom to discuss my financial situation honestly.
❑ I don't keep good business records.
❑ I didn't learn about money or how to plan ahead.
❑ I have no money to invest in my business.
❑ I don't really like to spend money on my business.
❑ It's too difficult for a woman to get a business loan.
❑ I have to earn a living; I can't afford to build my business.
❑ I hate to ask for money.
❑ I can't imagine having lots of money of my own.

❑ I have a poverty mentality.
❑ What good is it to be generous?

SESSION 2: EXHAUSTED AND OVERWHELMED

❑ I get tired of trying so hard all the time.
❑ Everyone else's needs overshadow mine.
❑ When do I get time for me?
❑ I'm so patient I become ineffective.
❑ I'm so stressed out.
❑ I feel like I'm on call all the time.
❑ I feel like I need to do everything myself.
❑ My kids need me, my husband needs me, my parents need me.
❑ I have a second job when I get home, taking care of everything.
❑ I need help and can't seem to find good help.
❑ I can't afford help.
❑ I have so much to do. I don't know what to do first sometimes.
❑ I'll never get everything done.
❑ I work so many hours for my business.
❑ I don't have time to sort it all out.
❑ I feel if I don't do it, who will?

SESSION 3: RELATIONSHIPS

❑ Everyone else's needs and interests seem to come before mine.
❑ I try too hard to please everyone.
❑ I overreact when clients/customers complain.
❑ I let clients and other business associates take advantage of me.
❑ I simply don't seem to be able to say no even when I know I should.

❑ I'm not good at delegating or asking for help.
❑ I make employees my friends and it causes me difficulties.
❑ I hate to fire anyone.
❑ I feel guilty when I tell family and friends I don't have time to talk or meet with them.
❑ People in my life do not respect my work or the fact that I am working.

SESSION 4: SEXISM

❑ I'm not comfortable dealing with men in business.
❑ I still feel like I'm expected to defer to men in business situations.
❑ I can't compete with men. They have more experience, contacts and business savvy.
❑ Many men in the business world don't take me seriously.
❑ There are different rules and expectations for men. It's easier for them.
❑ I've been the brunt of sexist remarks.
❑ I feel discriminated against in business.
❑ Men have wives to take care of them, to come home to.
❑ I think the male issue is always there.
❑ Men don't like women in their lives to move beyond them.

SESSION 5: FEARS AND ANXIETY ATTACKS

❑ I feel anxious and stressed out a lot of the time.
❑ I'm afraid of making the wrong decisions or choices.
❑ What if I do all this and don't succeed?
❑ I've failed before. It terrifies me to try again.
❑ When a customer or client is angry, I'm afraid my business is ruined forever.
❑ I'm afraid of looking foolish.
❑ I'm uncomfortable networking, asking for referrals, and soliciting new business.
❑ I worry a lot about what other business people think of me.

❏ I get terrified when I have to introduce myself or speak at a meeting.

❏ I don't think others take me seriously.

❏ Sometimes fear and anxiety paralyze me.

SESSION 6: THE GREAT PRETENDER ...THE ORGASM SYNDROME

❏ I pretend to be what I think people want me to be.

❏ I fake how I feel and think about many things.

❏ I pretend I'm not really smart so others will feel comfortable around me.

❏ I allow others to lead when I want to or think I should.

❏ I convince others I can do certain things when I know I can't.

❏ I feel like a fraud and I'm afraid of getting caught.

❏ I'm consistently nice and say, "Of course I'll do that."

❏ I pretend everything is wonderful when it isn't.

❏ I smile when I want to scream.

❏ I act agreeable when I disagree. I nod yes when I want to shake my head no.

❏ I agree to do things when I don't want to.

SESSION 7: NEGATIVE ATTITUDES

❏ Owning my own business is very hard. I often don't feel up to it.

❏ I don't want to do that.

❏ It takes too much time to do that.

❏ I don't like making business decisions.

❏ I just can't be bothered with all that.

❏ I want someone else to do certain things for me in my business so I don't have to.

❏ I'm not working with people I like.

❏ I can't focus on what I need to do.
❏ I get distracted easily.
❏ If I'm a success, I'll be all alone.
❏ It's her fault, it's his fault, it's my parents' fault. It's someone else's fault.
❏ It's just not easy for a woman.
❏ There's too much competition.
❏ I don't have enough experience, or training, or education.
❏ You have to look like "that" to be a winner.
❏ I'll never make a lot of money.
❏ I can't do that.
❏ I don't believe I can really be a success.

SESSION 8: BAD HABITS

❏ I know I don't exactly have it all together. It's the best I can do.
❏ I procrastinate when I don't know what to do.
❏ I procrastinate when I have to do something I don't want to do.
❏ I waste seemingly endless amounts of time with nonsense.
❏ I don't seem to be able to get organized.
❏ I have no business plan.
❏ I have no plan for dealing with unexpected business needs.
❏ My office is always a mess.
❏ I don't have time to be organized.
❏ I'm always late for meetings.
❏ I forget appointments.
❏ I forget to send thank-you notes/memos following important meetings.
❏ I lie about deadlines.
❏ I lie about why I don't get to a meeting or return calls.
❏ I make up lies or excuses for not doing certain things.

SESSION 9: SELF-ESTEEM

❑ I feel insecure, unsure of myself.
❑ I don't feel I'm enough: smart enough, pretty enough, thin enough, tall enough, good enough.
❑ I'm working on myself.
❑ I'm not sure I always know what I'm doing.
❑ I don't think I project a good professional image for my business.
❑ I'm too serious. I don't have a sense of humor when I know I should.
❑ I worry a lot about what others think of me.
❑ I have a difficult time dealing with powerful, rich, very successful people. Sometimes I feel insignificant or small with them.
❑ I'm always apologizing.
❑ I'm overly appreciative and grateful.
❑ I'll be blamed for everything that goes wrong.
❑ Everyone will abandon me if I don't do exactly what I think others want.
❑ I don't really feel a sense of passion or excitement about my business.

SESSION 10: WISHFUL THINKING

❑ I leave certain things to chance.
❑ I ignore signs of trouble.
❑ I act as if what I want to happen will, just because I want it to.
❑ I'll succeed only if it was meant to be.
❑ I don't listen to my instincts about people and situations.
❑ I trust other people will do right by me because I'm nice to them.
❑ I trust the universe will provide for me.
❑ I just hope and pray.
❑ I believe some things will just take care of themselves.
❑ I often think or say, "I'll deal with it tomorrow."

SESSION 11: DEALING WITH CRISES

- ❑ My business life feels like it's hanging on by a thread much of the time.
- ❑ I need a loan. My cash flow is terrible.
- ❑ I usually don't plan for change or the unexpected.
- ❑ My industry has changed a lot. I should have diversified long ago.
- ❑ I never plan for change.
- ❑ I have too much work and no one to help me.
- ❑ My staff is on vacation. I didn't plan their schedules to fit my needs.
- ❑ Losing one big client could ruin me.
- ❑ I need to learn to relax, to get better rest, to take care of myself.
- ❑ I have to keep pushing on, but I don't know how long I can keep this up.
- ❑ I need some time off.
- ❑ I don't give it much thought. I suppose the potential is always there for a crisis to hit.

SESSION 12: SUCCESS

- ❑ I need to identify my own vision of success and why I want to succeed in business.
- ❑ I need help identifying what I need and how to bring that into my business.
- ❑ I need to identify my business needs and concerns.
- ❑ I need a business plan.
- ❑ I need to improve my management skills.
- ❑ I need to learn to delegate.
- ❑ I need to identify what staff and help I need.
- ❑ I need to learn how to hire and fire staff.
- ❑ I need to do more networking, learn how to network, attend more networking meetings.

- ❑ I need to become an active member of business organizations.
- ❑ I need to expand my professional network.
- ❑ I need to improve my people skills and communicate more effectively.
- ❑ I would like to do public speaking as a way of promoting my business.
- ❑ I need help to improve my public speaking.
- ❑ I need to learn how to describe what it is I do.
- ❑ I need help preparing a business or marketing plan.
- ❑ I need to do public relations for my business or hire someone to do it.
- ❑ I know I need a mentor, advisor, or business therapist.

ACKNOWLEDGMENTS

I have wanted to be a writer of books since I was 14 years old. Through all the years of being a mother, a daughter, once upon a time a wife, a single mom, a mother-in-law, a grandmother, a god-mother, a friend, a volunteer, a business woman of many years, a business writer, a mentor, a dreamer, and a believer, I have also been an active and oftentimes passionate advocate of women's need to have financial security, economic independence, and a right to their own success.

We women also need the love and support of people who believe in us and who remind us to never give up. They assure us we have what it takes, they are willing to take risks with us and on our behalf, stay with us during the times of adversity, and rejoice with us during the happy times.

There are so many terrific women in my life whom I appreciate for their wisdom, friendship and generosity of spirit. These are the women who are my friends, the women I sit with on various boards for women, the women I meet at meetings, and the women I share some of my time and life with.

How very much I appreciate my dear friend and agent Carole Abel, who has been all of the above and more. She has listened to my ideas for books for so many years we could have filled a small library. She told me as I wrote this book to listen to my own voice and to use it. I did! I thank her with all my heart and soul. And how grateful I am to Carole and Walter, who so often give me a "room of my own."

Marcia Newfield and Nancy Swett helped me to bring clarity to my voice. Marcia is a suberb editorial critic who helped me navigate my way through the words and sentences as I wrote this book. Nancy helped my voice find a structure and organize the volume of pages of information and research I had collected. They provided wonderful and invaluable ideas and assistance. Thank you, thank you!

And thanks to a special woman who graces my life: Lucy Rosen, my friend for nearly 20 years who has shared her affection, talent, and belief in me. She and her daughter, my godchild, Sami, are very dear to me.

A few of the many other women who have supported me with their women-wise words and friendship throughout this challenging and wonderful adventure: Marsha Firestone, Lian Bloom, Tina Segal, Pamela Shenk, Jackie Goodwin, Rose Mancusi and Karen Christiansen.

I am thankful to the dozens of women I interviewed who trusted me, gave up their secrets and told me their stories.

To my daughter-in-laws, whom I am very fond of, Melynda Sylvester Rosen and Fay Greenfield Rosen, for their encouragement and for caring about me.

It is with a smile on my face that I extend my appreciation to my publisher, Chandler House Press and to the wonderful assistance and cooperation of the Director of Publishing, Claire Cousineau, who has given endlessly of her time and energy to help give this book its due.

There are, of course, the good men in my life. Friends and family who constantly remind me they believe in me, especially my long time friends Robert Raphael, Adrian Weissfeld, and David Eisenstadt.

However, it is my son Jory Rosen and my son Brett Rosen who, each in his own loving and—thank goodness!—very often humorous way, have shared their wisdom and hopefulness with me through the many years and the often circuitous path I have traveled to reach this wonderful place. I love them very much! Oh yes, I also thank three charming little boys, my grandsons, Jesse, Kyle, and Sean. Just because!

For my Dad and my Mom, who gave me a foundation of love.

Session I
Money

SESSION 1: MONEY

I Have Problems with Money and Money Is a Problem

Let's talk about your relationship with business, finance, and money

Even as we enter the 21st century, many women are often one paycheck away from poverty. Women's earnings average 74 cents to every dollar earned by men. Many women still have had little or no sense of entitlement about having a lot of money or even feeling comfortable at the thought of having it. Problems with money are much deeper and more diverse than just not having enough or wanting more. They involve all the attitudes inherited and self-generated thoughts that keep women away from their dreams and their potential, struggling to thrive, and oftentimes just to survive.

UNCOVERING THE SECRETS:
What Is There About Money You Don't Want to Talk About?

- ▶ I don't want anyone to know I'm struggling financially.
- ▶ I'm afraid of not getting a client or losing a client by asking to get paid or negotiating for what I want.
- ▶ Frequently I don't have enough money to pay my bills.
- ▶ My cash flow is horrible. I have no money saved. I didn't plan properly. I mishandled money. Now I'm terrified all the time.
- ▶ I can't get a loan or line of credit because I have bad credit.
- ▶ I'm really afraid of business failure and not being able to repay or recover money, even if I could get a loan.
- ▶ I believe in some way that money is the root of evil.

▶ If I'm too successful, bad things will happen to me or to someone I love and care about.

▶ I'm embarrassed to make more money than my father or my husband; I think it would hurt my relationship with them.

▶ I don't feel any man will love me if I'm successful and wealthy.

What are *your* money secrets?

THE SESSION

Getting Paid!

"How long has your client owed you this money?"

"Six months. I call them every Monday and ask them when they are going to send a check. They say I'm at the top of the list, or they expect to have money to pay me soon, or they just don't know."

"Do they ever promise they'll be sending you the money? Have you ever asked them to make a payment plan?"

"No and no."

"Did you have a signed contract with them?"

"Yes, but the payment schedule was rather loose because I had worked with them several times in the past, and I didn't want them to think I didn't trust them."

This is about business, not friendship. You always have to think about what you need to do to protect yourself and your business. Years ago many people agreed and followed through with a handshake. Maybe that worked then—and even then only for some people. Today, with everyone suing someone for something or other and businesses being so vulnerable, you have to be sure you're doing everything you can to protect your finances.

"Have you ever demanded they pay you within the next ten days or you'll send this to your attorney or take them to court? Are you independently wealthy so that you can write off this money?"

"Again, no and no."

This is Janice. She has owned her own small, moderately successful public relations agency for the past six years. She does a good job for her clients. She is good to her employees. She is also a good mom, wife, and daughter. In fact, she is so good she just smiles rather sweetly when people who owe her money tell her they can't pay right now. She hopes they will be good enough to pay some day soon. Inside she is actually boiling over, upset and distressed at her client's unwillingness to pay her what he owes. She is confused between wanting to be what she considers a good person and doing what she knows is the right thing to do at this point, that is, demand her money—or tell them she is turning it over to her attorney or a collection agency or taking them to small claims court.

I asked Janice if she could call this very late-paying client and tell them they need to send a check within the next five days or she will be turning this matter over to her attorney, that she has been very patient. They have been promising to pay her for weeks—actually months—and she no longer trusts their intention to pay her. Janice begins to turn a pale shade of green.

> "Can you do this? You earned the money. You deserve to be paid. You should not be dismissed and treated as if this is so insignificant. It's very important to you. Not only do you need the money, but it's yours; you earned it. It doesn't matter if you're going to take a trip to Hawaii with it or spend it on an Armani suit; it's your money."

> "I don't know if I can do that. What if they get angry?"

> "So what? Aren't you angry and upset?"

> "Yes. It's just that I get so nervous when I have to do something like this. I feel as if I'm bad, or this isn't what a good person should do. Not only won't they like me, what if they never hire me again?"

> "So what? Do you like working for free? Does everyone have to love you? Do you really need to feel as if everyone thinks you're wonderful?" I told Janice, "I don't think they think you're wonderful. I think they think they're doing a great job of manipulating you so they don't have to pay you.

"There are always exceptions to any rule. I've had people owe me money for a long time when I knew they were in financial trouble and we had always been friendly. I knew I could trust them to pay me. This isn't the situation. Also, there are times when someone will tell you they are having a cash flow problem and ask if they can make payments and then they do. This isn't the situation here either. These apparently are people who keep making promises they do not keep and give you false hope about possibly being paid soon. Every week for six months they have been making a promise and not keeping it, and you act as if you are thrilled they talk nicely to you when you call every Monday. Does it really make any sense?"

Today's businesswomen need to become financial role models for their children, their families, and future generations of women. Women need to make money a part of their consciousness and eliminate any stigma attached to being successful women. We need to spend time educating younger women about finances and the role of money in their lives. They need to have good information and clarity about the value and power of money. It's tough to be a role model or mentor when you're afraid to ask for money that someone owes you.

Again, I asked, "Do you really believe they're going to pay you? I know you hope they will. I know you believe that if you keep acting nicely enough, they'll come through. In the meantime, you begin each week not feeling very good about yourself or your business because of not taking the right actions and because you know what they're doing is lying to you and taking advantage of you."

I asked again, "Janice, can you pick up the phone right now and demand your money? Can you say you'll give them five days to pay or you're sending it to your attorney?"

What happens to Janice and so many women when they have to ask for money, collect money, and/or negotiate for money is that a

5

dialogue begins in their heads. "I want my money. I deserve it. I really have to get this money. What if they get nasty? What if they yell at me? God, I hope they say I can have a check today. It's my money; they better pay me. What if I make them angry and they never pay me? What if they never want me to work for them again?"

I understand Janice's dialogue and her concerns: either collect your money or feel as if they love you because you're such a good and kind person. She probably can't have both with these people. If she demands to be paid, she will have her money and her self-respect. In fact, she might even have the respect of the client. This need to be Miss Good and Loved by Everyone is not acceptable behavior and certainly is detrimental to her business. Treating people with dignity and respect is important, but equally important is being treated with dignity and respect.

Janice is still stuck in her limiting mindset about money. Her money issue is certainly connected to her fear issue. Sometimes, one issue has an impact on several others. This is particularly so with the money issue: fear of being too successful or not successful enough, fear that if you make a lot of money you are taking it away from someone else. Janice is still taking baby steps, but that's better than none at all. She faxes reminders that money is due. Calling is still too stressful for her. She now asks her clients to sign a simple agreement at the beginning of a project, and she even asks for a retainer—most of the time. She's making progress, and there's a lot to be said for that.

Whenever a woman lets someone take advantage of her, intimidate her, or abuse her by his or her behavior or attitude, she diminishes herself. It may seem easy, or at least familiar, to surrender to feeling helpless and hopeless, but that's bound to have a negative impact on her and her business.

I know, I know, every situation is different. Once when I signed a contract for a project with a pharmaceutical company and two other women from the agency were with me to discuss the overall concept and implementation of the project, we had a very unnerving moment about money. The contract was for $30,000 and one of the department heads who had joined us, along with the manager who had hired us, commented when we were presented with the contract and the check, "Now each of you has $10,000 to go out shopping for new clothes." I was absolutely stunned as well as furious. At that moment the dialogue in my head was "Do I tell him he has a lot of nerve, I have a business to run, employees to pay? Do I smile and ignore the comment? How do I get out of here without him knowing I am furious?" All I could say at the time was "My agency is very pleased to have this opportunity to work with you."

I've thought about that incident many times over the years, wishing I had said a lot of different things. Yet I know, today more than ever, you have to pick your fights. What fight are you willing to take on and for what reason? I knew by his behavior and attitude there was no way I could educate this particular person that women need money for the same reasons as men do. I had the money. He was annoyed. I still had the money. However, wherever and whenever we can, women must give out the message that women do need money for the same reasons as men do.

GAINING CONTROL OF YOUR BUSINESS FINANCES

Sarah had to negotiate a contract. We spoke every day throughout the process. When we first met, I asked Sarah if she knew what she wanted the outcome to be from these negotiations. She was negotiating a yearlong contract with a big client. They had a lot of financial and legal power, and she needed not only to establish fees and schedules, but also to protect herself regarding payment and responsibilities. "I know I want to charge what is fair to me and not be expected to take on added responsibilities without added remuneration." To her credit, she respected herself, and she requeste fair payment and reasonable time frames.

"Have you written out a list of the outcomes you would like to
have from these negotiations?"

"No."

"Would you be willing to do that, and we both can review
and discuss it?"

And she did! I also wanted to review the contract and have her
show it to an attorney.

"Do you want someone to go with you to the negotiating
meeting?"

"No, I don't want them to feel I don't trust them or that they
might have trouble with me as the project progresses."
Understandable: her position made perfect sense. "I've
worked with them in the past and they've always been
very fair. This is just so much bigger and so much more
work, I'll need to hire a part-time assistant to work with me
on this project. I want to be sure we understand each other
and accept each other's ground rules."

"Can you tell them what you just told me?"

"Yes, in a way. Mostly, when I'm getting ready for a meeting, I
get butterflies in my stomach. I'm afraid I'll say something
or ask for something that will ruin my chances for getting
the contract."

"What do you think might happen?"

"Well, it's not so much about the money. I don't want them to
feel I'm not grateful for this opportunity."

"Do you believe you have a lot to offer this project and this
company? Do you believe you have the skills and the
expertise to handle this project?"

"Absolutely."

"Good, I do too. I don't think they would have invited you to
participate in such a big project if they didn't believe in
your qualifications. It's nice you appreciate the opportunity, but I would go cautiously on showing gratitude. You
have something they want and need. It's a business
arrangement and you're equals. They have the money and

you have something they wish to purchase. Keep in mind that gushing gratitude can be quite annoying."

I used to gush appreciation a lot—until one time a male friend and business associate of mine told me to cut it out, that I was equal to the people I meet and who hire me. I always knew it; it just helped to hear it. Now I want you to hear it. If I find myself beginning to be in the gushing mode, I literally start talking to myself. "Are you crazy, Marcia? You sound like they've just shown you the Hope Diamond. Calm down. Remember who you are, what you have to offer. You're their equal. Stop it! Stop it now!" It helps a lot to remind myself.

Sarah also knew she was an equal. "Something just starts swimming around in my head." Ah yes, the internal dialogue takes up residence once again. Her dialogue has been going on since she was asked to present a proposal. Once she received word she had the project, the dialogue became a full-blown internal conversation. Something like: "I love the idea of having this project. I wonder if it's too much for me. They like me so much now. What if I mess up? That would be upsetting. Will they pay me what I proposed? What if they want to pay me less? I don't want less. I will more than earn what I'm asking. I do excellent work. I'm very reliable. What if they become angry with me? What if they decide not to hire me? Maybe I should settle for less money. Then they won't expect so much." This is not a very productive dialogue. In fact, it causes much angst.

"Sarah, stop it! This is nonsense; tell the voice in your head to take a long nap. I think you need to write down what you want and rehearse what you're going to say to them. The more prepared you are, the easier it will be. You shouldn't have to settle. I know you trust your skills and talent. So do I. You are terrific at what you do. What's really going on here?"

"It's not very ladylike to negotiate for money. The truth is it feels like that's a man's thing. On some level I think I shouldn't have to be involved in that aspect of business. I mean, I love the creativity and the planning. The money and negotiating make me feel like I'm expected to be so tough. If I act tough, they won't like me. If I'm not tough enough, I'll never get what I want. I hate those comments men make about tough-acting women. I'm not sure how to respond or handle the situation."

"So you would rather they like you than pay you what you're worth? How about coming to work for me? I'll be glad to like you a lot and pay you much less! As for how to respond or handle a situation where someone comments on your being tough, I suggest that you always be prepared with a few appropriate comments that take you off the defensive. First of all, never apologize for asking for what you want. Next, if you are tough yet comfortable in your communication, and firm without sounding harsh, chances are you won't have those comments. In fact, they will respect your negotiating skills."

"I know how silly this sounds; of course I want the money. I just find it difficult to work with people who don't like me a lot."

"Sarah, this is not a personality contest. They are hiring you because of your skills and talent. True, they want to hire someone they are comfortable working with. I'm not suggesting you go in and demand in some harsh, unpleasant tone that you want what you requested. I am suggesting you gently and firmly state that you understand that they have a budget to deal with and you respect their need to negotiate. However, for you to do the best job for them will require many hours, and you have to be compensated in order to deliver what they expect. Perhaps there are even one or two other points in the contract you can negotiate to show you are fair and willing to be a team player.

"Let's discuss what those points might be. One thing is certain. I don't want you to overcompensate. Don't promise more than you can really deliver just so they will hire you. Don't agree to complete the project in less time than is realistic for you. Call me before you go to the meeting, and then call me when you can after the meeting. You need the same support systems working with you as they do."

Sarah called me before she went to her meeting for a brief rehearsal for what she was going to ask for and how she would respond to their concerns about money in particular. I gave her some talking points. 'This is my fee. This is what I can do for that fee. I appreciate your budget constraints; however, I am unable to do what you are requesting for less money. I want to do the best job possible for you. I could spread the project over more months and less hours per month. This is how I am compensated. I am paid a retainer and then monthly payments on set dates. This is the time frame for the project. I'm confident I can help you achieve your objectives.'

Sarah wanted to win this client. She followed the talking points, stood her ground, and came away with a signed contract, a check, and a wonderful feeling. Me too!

I work with women all the time who have friends they call or business associates they partner with on various projects so they can have just that type of support network to help them through a problem. Negotiating for money can be very difficult, certainly stressful, and even upsetting if you're not accustomed to the process. It can also be daunting even if you have done it before.

Just remember that using this as an excuse stops you from acting out of the right attitude and achieving what you keep saying you want. People can get into power plays, and sometimes their need to win takes priority over being reasonable. The more support you have around to help you deal with the negotiations and the personalities involved, the easier it will be for you. The more prepared you are for these negotiations, the better chance you'll have of a successful outcome.

INVESTING MONEY IN YOUR BUSINESS

Money or lack of it is an enormous issue for women. The objective reasons are numerous. No matter. I've heard all the excuses dozens of times. "I don't charge enough." "I hate to ask for money." "I don't want to call them for payment." "I dislike negotiating." "It's very difficult to borrow money for my business." "I hate dealing with the money part of the business." One of my favorites used to be "What if I make more money than my parents (usually meaning "father") or my husband?"

Throughout my years of working with women, I have continually found they have a difficult time spending money to grow their businesses. They will invest in their homes, their children, their clothes, reshaping and remaking the way the look. Still, they continue to find it hard to invest in their businesses. It's as if they have no right to invest in something that can make them successful and financially secure. After all, we women are used to receiving compliments on how lovely we look, what good children we have, what a beautiful home we have. Rarely have we been treated to phrases and praises for great business decisions. "Marcia, you have an excellent head for business; your thinking is so strong and logical. I'm impressed by how you negotiated that project. You're so good at what you do." Well, someone has to tell us in order for us to grow confidence.

It's easy to understand why women have become so uncomfortable (and downright frightened) that they make all sorts of excuses. Yet, I strongly believe they don't fear the failure as much as they fear the success. They fear the visibility and the responsibility. They fear being seen or told they're so much of a show-off.

The reasons are reasonable; the excuses are unacceptable.

The new entrepreneurial women want a serious place in the success column and, in order to get it, they need to have a healthier relationship with money than the majority of women who have traveled this road before them. Women have to be willing to talk to bankers and other financial people and make them part of their support system.

I organized the curriculum for a 10-week entrepreneurial training course, Succeeding in Business. There were a few men in the class; most were women. They ranged from thinking about what kind of business they wanted to start, to having just started one, to having been in business for several years. Money was an issue for just about every one of them.

Katrina told me she wanted to go to a bank and get a start-up loan. Joanna wanted to borrow money to help with her cash flow. My first question to each of them: "Do you have any collateral?" My second question: "Do you have a business plan?" Without collateral it's nearly impossible to get a traditional loan unless someone with good collateral is willing to cosign for you. Plus, when you go to a bank, a private investor, or even a member of your family to ask for a loan, it's important—in fact, in most cases, absolutely essential—to have a business plan.

Katrina said she had some collateral and believed she could get a cosigner if necessary. Joanna had neither. That doesn't mean she should give up her dream. It just required different thinking and reviewing other possibilities.

I told each of them how they could get help writing their business plans through various business organizations such as the Small Business Administration. There are now many economic development groups available in nearly every state to offer hands-on advice—usually for free or a modest cost. There are state and county departments for women's business development.

The business plan is the practical and written version of your business, complete with anticipated expenses and income. Ah, sounds too simple. So is dieting, I'm told!

I find that most of the time I mention writing a business plan, it's as if I am suggesting jumping from a bridge. The terrified look of confusion or frustration says it all: "How do I do this while I run my business or continue to earn a living? I need the money now." Or "Why bother? No one will loan me money. My credit is awful. Or "I have no one who can help me financially. Also, I can't write."

How else can you get money? Many women have built successful businesses on the strength of their credit cards. Not my all-time favorite option, but it has worked for many an entrepreneur if they have the courage to take the risk and the willingness to be very responsible with how they use this method. There are angel and venture capital groups all over the country. They too want a business plan.

There are numerous resources for obtaining financial resources including the Business Women's Network in Washington, DC. Their WOW book offers many facts, as well as information about financial resources. The National Chamber of Commerce for Women in New York offers 101 reports on how you can get money for your business. You can get a free three-page sample *Money Finding Report.* Also from the Chamber you can order the book *How to Get Money: Hot Tips, Cold Cash & 2001 Other Cool Financing Strategies.* (Call 212 685-3454 for more information on these materials.) Also check with your local chamber and the local chapter of your industry organization as well as the resources section of this book.

Sometimes it's just too overwhelming for some women. Sometimes the best strategy to begin with is to write a one- or two-page action plan. Highlight your goals and the actions required to achieve those objectives and list potential expenses and income.

Katrina had some money saved from her job and was hoping to start a business selling handmade scarves, vests, and other items produced overseas. She was able to buy them at a very reasonable cost and was confident she had a good market for the items. She had done her homework, talked to stores that might carry the items, considered home sales, and eventually planned to open a small boutique where she would expand her line. She needed money to buy the product and market the product. She had a good idea. She had plenty of positive enthusiasm and energy. She did not have lots of money, and what she had she needed to spend carefully.

She was not feeling in a panic and was being very thoughtful about the best way to secure a business loan. She had purchased a couple of books and booklets on how to write a plan. I told her I would review the plan for her and that she should consider hiring an accountant to assist with the financial elements of the plan.

I constantly ask women I work with to consider this important business plan as a road map that they can follow to help them build their businesses. Remember: viability and vision. True, it's usually about the money first; however, the plan can be invaluable in directing the day-to-day operation of the business, as well as its future growth. It can help you by giving you guidelines for planning, budgeting, using marketing strategies, and taking advantage of expansion opportunities.

All of this makes a lot of sense. Yet most women will tell you attempting to secure a loan is almost as difficult as childbirth. Well, not quite, but close. It is indeed easier today for women than 20 or 30 years ago. Hey, it's easier than 10 years ago. Of course, 50 years ago it was nearly impossible, but that's another story. Yet many women would rather face a firing squad than a banker, a well-to-do relative, or investors.

Many years ago, I walked into what was then called "The Women's Bank" in New York and asked to meet with a bank representative so I could learn what they did to help women. "Actually nothing," she said. "We can give a loan only if you have collateral or a cosigner." I still haven't figured out what they were all about. They don't even exist anymore. They may have understood money; they didn't understand public relations or marketing. I've found in conversations with many women who attended the numerous classes and seminars I presented at American Women's Economic Development and Business Outreach Centers that women and money was an almost taboo subject.

I read a wonderful quote in *Vogue* magazine recently: "Men bring money to the table; women bring beauty. I think it's a better deal for the man. Earning potential only increases with age. Beauty fades." Women now have the opportunity to bring money to the table, and they are beginning to understand its power.

As for Katrina, she finally secured her business loan. She deserved to. Joanna finally gave up. I wish she hadn't.

Women have to be able to cope with the unaccustomed visibility and responsibilities, both personal and social, that wealth, power, and a "portfolio of one's own" bring. By debunking the myths and providing a new belief system for acquiring, using, and celebrating the power of money, women will begin to be less reluctant to have success and wealth and to take on the challenges that are imposed by such a delightful situation.

THE SOLUTIONS

Money can go a long way toward setting a woman free. I've been an advocate of women's financial success and economic independence for many years. With money of her own, a woman can be free of worry from financial security, free of dependency, free of tasks she'd rather not do, and free of the constraints imposed by traditional social roles. She's free to support causes she cares about and influence the world we live in. She's able to help provide for her children and protect them. Over the last half century, especially the last 20 years, women entrepreneurs making their own money have been one of the greatest factors in our undeniably increasing political influence and in our major impact on the economy.

With all money has to offer a woman, why do so many women still have MindBlocks against it? Why do so many women still not take the steps necessary to ensure their financial success and security? Why do women demand, expect, and accept less than they should? Why are so many women frequently in a perpetual . state of distress about money matters? How can women move beyond their fear and embarrassment regarding money problems so they can ask for and get help?

MindBlocks are often the response to the realistic RoadBlocks that women encounter in the business world. These are obstacles that can deter women and interfere with their success. Money RoadBlocks—such as access to capital, debt, equal pay for equal work in the corporate world, lack of money due to divorce, and not being taken seriously by vendors, clients, and customers—all contribute to the limiting mindsets, attitudes, and behaviors regarding money.

Only within the last 20 years has a foundation for women's business success really been laid. We need to have practical solutions to eliminate the RoadBlocks. We need to ask for help, be connected to good people, challenge our negative thinking, move beyond our history, and build on our talents and successes to eliminate the MindBlocks.

I urge you to resolve now that having your own money and being financially successful is important to you. Women, like men, are in business to earn a living and take pride in their accomplishments. If you have symptoms and secrets about money that limit you, create a plan of action to free yourself from limiting mindsets such as the poverty mentality or "success won't happen to me." Own up to your money MindBlocks and RoadBlocks. What are they? Write them down in your journal, talk about them with a trusted friend or advisor, highlight the ones in this book that apply to you, invest in one of the new excellent books or seminars now available about women and money. You're worth it!

Solutions to money problems for women entrepreneurs usually fall into four major categories:

- ▶ Examine your relationship with money.
- ▶ Gain control of your finances.
- ▶ Get paid.
- ▶ Invest in your success.

Examine Your Relationship with Money

Traditional Value Conflicts

Examine your beliefs about money, especially as they relate to your identity as a woman. Traditional values were that women didn't work outside the home and depended on men for their needs. For some women, that's still the way it is, either for practical or emotional reasons. However, many women today are pursuing independent ambitions and business success.

Love, Men, and a Woman's Success

Do you worry men will find you unappealing because you are financially successful or that your relationship with your partner will be destroyed by your success? Money certainly can change you and your life. Involve the men in your life in the transformation. You assume that men, or your partner, will feel threatened. But also how will it make you feel?

Discuss your concerns with your partner. It's the best way to protect your relationship. Don't assume your husband or boyfriend won't be proud of you and glad for the financial advantage. Many women are pleasantly surprised by their partners' support. How are you going to ensure that you have enough time for each other? Make dates with each other. Talk openly and honestly about money. Go to couples therapy if necessary. Respect your differences and try to be supportive of the other person's life choices. *Real men like smart, successful women.*

Fathers and Other Male Relatives

Along the same lines, are you worried about what it would do to your relationship with your male relatives to be more successful than they? If any of them have been helpful to you in becoming an entrepreneur, acknowledge them. Let them know how they've helped. Just know that sometimes your success will be OK with them and sometimes it won't.

Money: Not the Root of Evil

Money is not the root of all evil. It can do you a lot of good—it can also do good for the people in your life you love, your community, and causes you care about. You may need to give up some of your martyrdom and sacrifice to feel entitled to money. But, so what?

Fears and Embarrassment

- Don't bury your head in the sand.
- Take an honest look at your business financials.
- Are your fears justified?
- Are your fears exaggerated?

▶ Get professional advice.

Gain Control of Your Finances

Get Good Advice

▶ Bad financial advice is going to get you into a heap of trouble. It's very important to get the right advice! You want objective, competent, qualified advice from a certified financial planner or accountant. If you don't already have someone like that on your team, you can easily find one by getting referrals from other successful people or from your banker or by interviewing consultants listed in your local phone book. If you're networking, someone in your professional groups may be able to provide you with a referral.

▶ If you feel you're not getting the service you need in the manner you would like from a financial advisor, fire him or her and find someone else.

▶ Don't let anyone intimidate you about money issues. You have a right to know.

Educate Yourself About Money

▶ You have to take responsibility and be accountable for your business financials. Even if you have accountants, bookkeepers, and advisors, you have to manage the money on some level.

▶ Take a seminar or college course.

▶ Read up on business administration, investing, and money management.

▶ Join an investment club.

▶ Visit online financial resources.

▶ Subscribe to one of the consumer finance magazines.

▶ I want to remind you, again, there are several excellent books and seminars available about women and money.

► Ask your advisor for help with any concept, information, or practice you may not understand or be familiar with.

► Take charge! It's your business! It's your financial well-being!

Keep Good Records and Stay Up to Date on Your Finances

► Keep track of your income and expenses.

► Be aware of your cash flow.

► Read and understand statements and reports from banks, investments, insurance policies, etc. Call about questions and correct errors promptly.

► Review all bills carefully.

Save!

► Save a small percentage of all income. Savings will alleviate anxiety about money and give you some breathing room.

Debt and Bankruptcy

► Too much debt is crippling from both a practical and emotional standpoint. If you have too much debt or feel you are consistently spending more than your income permits and heading for trouble, get help.

► There are many nonprofit debt consolidation programs available to the consumer. Check with your attorney, accountant, or local office of the Small Business Administration. Call one and get started on the road to financial repair.

► Bankruptcy should be your last resort, but an option you should not necessarily dismiss. It doesn't have to cost a lot to process, you don't have to lose everything, and in time and with effort your credit can be repaired. Most bankruptcy attorneys do the same thing. Call four or five in your area and ask about fees, payment schedule, and time it takes to complete the process.

▶ Give up the embarrassment about it. Former President Harry Truman filed for bankruptcy—and look what he accomplished afterward.

Get Paid

How Much Should You Be Charging Your Clients/Customers?

▶ Plan to periodically check up on what people in your business charge. It may change over time.

▶ Contact several other people in your industry, preferably people who are not in direct competition with you, and ask what they get for what they do. Call other cities or go online and find people in your industry you can ask. There are always good people willing to share this information with you.

▶ Ask for information from advisors in business organizations— the U.S. Small Business Administration (SBA) branch offices, SCORE (Service Corps of Retired Executives), your trade group—about what fees or prices you can charge.

▶ If you can afford it, hire someone to research it for you. A business consultant, career counselor, or financial advisor may provide this service to you. Agree in advance on their methods and fees, and get a final written report.

▶ Figure out what you need to earn to meet your expenses. Don't forget money for savings, insurance, retirement, vacation, and sick days, in addition to other business overhead. You may need to add in your personal living expenses. Women with financial responsibilities at home may want to add in money for home-related services like housecleaning, property maintenance, and childcare. Take a good hard look at what you must earn compared with the going rate for your type of business. You may need to make adjustments upwards or downwards.

▶ Do a reality check and adjust accordingly. Are you charging enough? Are you charging too much?

▶ Don't settle for less. Expect the most.

Expect to Get Paid—and Paid on Time

► Create an agreement or a set of agreements for your business and get them signed by customers before performing work. The agreement process is an invaluable opportunity for discussing payment arrangements, including when you will be paid, how much you will be paid, and for what. The agreement should also spell out what will occur if aspects of the agreement, such as full and timely payment, are not met. Never assume the other party understands or agrees to anything unless you discuss it and get it in writing. Legally, you have more power with a written, signed agreement if the other party fails to meet the terms.

► To develop your own agreement, there are excellent books available on legal agreements for virtually any industry. At a minimum, they are a good place to start. Visit your local library or go online to find the right information.

► Hire a lawyer to help you draw up an agreement. Get a referral to a good lawyer, preferably one who understands your business and its particular pitfalls. To reduce legal fees, do your homework first: consider having a lawyer review an agreement that you draft instead of creating an agreement from scratch.

► Contact businesses similar to yours in other geographic regions and ask them to fax you a sample agreement or discuss legal pitfalls with you.

► It's standard in most service businesses to get retainers or deposits in advance of performing work. The retainer or deposit should be paid with the signed contract. Protect your interests. It's foolish not to.

► For retail businesses, set ground rules for accepting or not accepting payment by check. Your banker can help you set up protection systems.

► Never extend more credit than you're prepared to lose. Sometimes it may be appropriate to take risks to get certain business in the door. You need to decide what degree of risk is comfortable and appropriate.

► Sometimes an effective way to get paid in advance for certain types of work is to offer incentives or discounts.

► Send your billing out on time. Allow two to four weeks before payment is due unless you've made different arrangements. Make getting paid a priority.

► When payment is late, take immediate action. Call the customer to discuss it. Refer to your agreement. You should be assured that payment is on its way and that your agreement will be met in the future.

► If you have a phobia about confronting delinquent customers yourself, consider hiring someone to handle your accounts receivable for you, even if you have only two accounts. Have someone make the call posing as your bookkeeper. If it's a bigger task, hire a collection agency to handle your accounts receivable.

► Sometimes a customer tries to string you along. They may not take your calls. They may outright refuse to pay. Your options are to scream at them, give up, or get satisfaction through other means, such as an attorney or a collection service. Do whatever is in your own best interests. You have to negotiate with yourself at times like this: is the amount of time and money it's going to take you to collect this money going to cost too much?

► Another essential: keep good business records.

Invest in Your Business

Invest in Professional Help

► Over time, build a professional team of consultants made up of a financial advisor, a lawyer, and a business consultant.

► Add people who offer value, expertise, or the ability to increase volume.

▶ Develop strategic alliances that are mutually beneficial. There are times you can provide each other with services needed and save expenditures.

Invest in New Services, Facilities, and Equipment

▶ Identify what new services, facilities, and equipment would help grow your business.

▶ Read your industry publications: who offers special price packages and special services of value to you?

▶ Be alert to trends and new products and services in demand in your industry.

▶ It's worth shopping around for the best price. If you don't have the time, this is something you can delegate. Tell your mother or friends to stop calling you and start making calls to help you!

Pursue Financing and Investors

▶ Spend time and money to get financing and to pursue investors if you have a project or concept that needs funding. That means being prepared with a business plan.

▶ If you can't afford to pay your accountant or a business consultant to help you develop the plan, there are nonprofit organizations that can help you. Start with your local branch of the Service Corps of Retired Executives (SCORE), which is associated with the SBA. They also have considerable funds available for small business loans, especially for women! They are often aware of other funding resources. Ask them.

▶ Contact women's organizations, such as Women Incorporated or the National Chamber of Commerce for Women. They both offer information on access to capital.

▶ Your banker, accountant, or financial planner can advise you of other financing options or possibly connect you to investors.

MY STORY

I have memories of those moments when I let opportunities simply get lost. It felt like they slipped through my fingers. They were there and then gone. What really happened was I was not prepared to deal with those opportunities. I was always good at eliminating certain RoadBlocks. For me the MindBlocks have always been the stumbling blocks, those limiting mindsets that I let control my early business career and, in fact, much of my life.

I always thought I should be able to live my life doing whatever it was I wanted to, the same as a man could. I was raised to believe I was smart and capable and full of potential. Only the other message I was given was that I had to be careful not to "get in trouble." Also, that men don't like women who are smarter or do better than them at certain things, like sports or making money. And I bought into these messages as well. Throughout my adult life, I was constantly at odds with myself over which side of the coin meant more to me. I learned to love and excel in the world of business and I also wanted to have love, a family and be loved. Go figure: I wanted it all. Some nerve!

All my friends married before I did and I was married at the ripe old age of nearly 22. Almost all my friends planned their careers to be housewives and mothers. I remember when one of our friends said she was going to go to law school. When she walked away from us, we commented, "Who will ever want to marry her if she does?" She did go to law school. She did get married. I doubt she ever knew how wonderful I thought that was and how envious I was that her family gave her permission to go for it as few women of the '50s did.

My first business, which I actually started on a wing and a prayer when I was in my early 20s, was a nursery school. It was suggested I send my rather bright and curious four-year-old to a more formal nursery school than the one I had him in. (OK. So he figured out how to unlock a gate and let all the kids out onto a busy street!)

At any rate, there was no school available for him and someone suggested I start my own. What did I know? Sounded like a good idea to me. So I did. I called an artistic friend and asked her if she would go into business with me. And before I knew it, we had rented space in the mornings that was used in the afternoons as a nursery school and suddenly we were running a small nursery school of our own. The first year I picked up and drove home at least half of the 19 students we had. My friend ultimately moved away, I got another partner, and some 10 years later I owned two schools with close to 200 children.

It was the early '60s. My friends used to be sorry for me that I "had to work" and my mom used to say when I got home, "Oh good, now you can take a nap." I didn't need a nap. The most important lessons I learned during those years was that I had the ability and instincts to be a successful entrepreneur and to earn good money. I had found my calling.

Sometime over the last couple of years of my owning these schools, someone came to me with a plan suggesting I franchise my nursery schools. He understood marketing, presented me with a marketing strategy, and knew that what I had developed could be successfully repeated across the country. Some years later others would do just that. For me, without the support of other people in my life, having two young sons and not anywhere near enough sense of self to explore the offer further, I let the opportunity pass.

The fact that I understood only the of marketing as it affected building my own schools is such an irony, since one of my strongest skills now is my ability to develop successful marketing strategies for businesses and nonprofit organizations. The opportunity passed. I sold my nursery schools and moved with my family to a new city. Once in a while I think about those days and that missed opportunity. Mostly I value how I learned to be in business, something few women of my generation knew or even began to explore until the last quarter of this century.

You would think missing one opportunity would be enough for me. Unfortunately, there was a second. I started a public relations/marketing agency in New Mexico. Within a little over two years it was the second largest agency in the state and I had a staff of 14, including my dad, who came to work for me to both help and protect me.

He saw I had something terrific growing but at the same time I was sinking emotionally because of difficult relationship issues. I was so proud of what I had accomplished with my business and involvement in the community and at the same time I was my struggling to keep things under control. I wanted to be a terrific parent, keep my marriage intact, and build a successful business. I emerged from the stress of these struggles divorced and selling my business. However, I was left with a deep awareness of how strong I really was and the incredible opportunity I had created for myself.

I have made a lot of money over the years. I've always felt this is quite an accomplishment for a woman who came out of the '50s. So how did I find myself after many years in business in serious financial trouble? Let me tell you, it was very troubling. I felt foolish and miserable and I really just wanted to stomp my feet like a three-year-old. I found myself saying, "I want what I want and I want it now!" Very adult.

I had left much of the financial control of my business to others, which would have been fine if I had also maintained strong management and accountability for the money. But I had "dropped the ball" because I felt I couldn't do or handle everything. So I was complicit by my negligence and also responsible for the problems that resulted. I was determined to overcome this adversity, no matter what, no matter how long. I finally told the people handling my money that "the rules of the game have changed" and I took charge. Goodbye MindBlocks!

It is one of the reasons why I'm so adamant about women and money, about the need for women to be accountable for their financial life, about the need for all women to have money of their own and economic security.

PARTING WORD

Start envisioning what you want. Eliminate your money Mind-Blocks and RoadBlocks.

Session 2

Exhausted and Overwhelmed

SESSION 2: EXHAUSTED AND OVERWHELMED

Sometimes It's All Just Too Much

Let's talk about what you do and expectations you place on yourself

No, you really can't do it all yourself. It's too much. Women need to know how to ask for help, expect to get good help and support, and also know there's a time to just say no. We have for too long accepted the burden of being so nice and so good that we are exhausted and overwhelmed more often than not. So what if everyone doesn't love you or think you're wonderful or comment on how terrific you are? When we take on so much more than we can and should, we become not only exhausted and overwhelmed. We become resentful, angry, and even depressed. This is not a good tradeoff.

UNCOVERING THE SECRETS:
What's Really Causing You to Feel So Exhausted and Overwhelmed?

- ▶ I'm embarrassed to ask for help; everything is such a mess.
- ▶ I don't want anyone to know how close I am to falling apart.
- ▶ I know I should say no. Sometimes I just can't. I feel like a "yes addict."
- ▶ I'm not sure what help I need or where to begin.
- ▶ I love being praised for being wonderful.
- ▶ I cave in to pressures and expectations.
- ▶ I don't really know how to negotiate with the people in my life to ask for what I need and want. I don't know how to negotiate with myself so I can keep a balance in my life, so I can be a success and still enjoy my life and be happy.

What are *your* secrets?

30

THE SESSION

What About Me?

Asking for What I Need

Getting Help

Planning, Preparation, and Proper Organization

Why is it that when a woman says she is exhausted, depleted, has had it, can't do it all, it's expected she should consider giving up her business or career and return to the home and hearth?

Why is it we are often asked to give up that which most nurtures us to nurture others even more than we have done and already do?

> "It's just too much," offered Rachel. "When I come home from my business at the end of each day, I begin my second job. The kids want attention, my husband expects dinner, my parents want to visit, and my friends want to chat. There's just not enough time to do it all. I feel overwhelmed and stressed. Forget any love life with my husband. I collapse into bed, I'm so exhausted!"

Rachel is certainly pushing herself and often is overwhelmed by the pressure of so many responsibilities. As a mother of a young child, Rachel takes care of her little one, runs her business, and works hard to have a good relationship with her husband. "I realized I couldn't do it all. Your suggestion was good, that I make a list of what I do at home and what I need help with and then negotiate with my husband who does what and when. We have begun to negotiate what each of us is responsible for doing in the home, with our daughter, and how to find quality time for each other."

One step at a time we reviewed what she needed most: help cleaning the house, additional help driving her daughter to and from daycare, a part-time employee to handle filing and making calls. We found someone in her community who could clean, she asked her husband to drive an extra day a week, and she started

31

someone just one half day a week to help with office work. Now she's working her way up to two half days. The more she asks for and accepts help, hires good people, even if it's just a few hours a week, the less overwhelmed she feels. She is making more money by spending her business time being productive.

When Rachel and I first discussed her situation, we agreed that it's helpful in general for a woman to have negotiating skills. A couple has to have a good and loving relationship and want to keep it together in order to negotiate with each other. We agreed that some women would rather end the relationship. Some keep it only because of finances: "I love my husband, I want this to work out."

We laughed at speculating why any man would offer to do his share of the housework and childcare if he could come home, put his feet up, and be served. They just don't think the way we women do. It may be societal; it may be they had mothers who waited on them hand and foot; it may be they think it's women's work. However, any good man, when faced with the daunting tasks facing a working woman, will acknowledge he should share in the day-to-day responsibilities. Hopefully. One day, Rachel's husband told her he understood what she was doing and how important her business was to her, that he wanted her to be a success and was glad to share that with her.

She has always said he's one of the good guys. "I'm lucky to have found someone who thinks what I want to do is important. We probably will have to keep negotiating and renegotiating, but at least he is open and willing."

Rachel's story is a success. She has good energy and a good relationship with her husband. She truly values him and their relationship. And she will have to keep renegotiating. As her business grows and as her daughter grows, their lives and needs will change. What's more, Rachel or any woman feeling overwhelmed and exhausted has to look at negotiating with herself. I have a friend who told me she does this all the time, prioritizing and balancing her life each and every day based on her own values.

As I write this session, I'm thinking about a movie I really want to see, preferably later today. However, writing this book is my priority. I negotiated with myself that if I accomplished a certain amount of work by late afternoon, I would go to that movie. Like my friend, I also negotiate with myself frequently. What am I willing to do to bring certain things I want and need into my life on a daily basis? I say NO a lot to people who drain my energy and my time. What are you willing to do to bring what you want into your life? Who are you willing to bring in to help you?

Have you learned to say NO? I'm always amazed at how we women make other people's needs and desires more important than our own.

We have to know every single day—and I am convinced of this—that we are just as important and must say NO when we want to, need to, and must. NO is like your shield of protection, especially from the type of people I feel are like vampires who willingly suck you of your strength and success by asking too much of you too often.

Some women do it to themselves by isolating themselves and refusing to ask for help. Some women just don't know how to move forward out of that mindset. Others are so familiar with one way they prefer to stay in the "muck and mess" and complain about it to anyone who will listen. That's great for getting attention. We all know someone like that.

Caroline spends a lot of time complaining to anyone who will listen.

"If only someone would come and help me. I need someone to organize me, to help me every day, only I can't afford it. In fact I'm so embarrassed at what a mess things are here, I can't even imagine what it would be like to let someone come into my office."

From year to year I have heard the same story from her. I've told her many times to bring someone in to help a few hours at first. That could free her up to bring in more business and ultimately more money. Or she could work with that person each week and begin to organize her business and most likely her life. I suggested she might also ask one of her friends or business associates to do a trade with her. Caroline is in a service business and could work out an arrangement that would be mutually beneficial. I told her that I've done that many times. I get help and it feels great to have a sense of not being alone.

Whatever suggestion I've made, she's said she either had tried it already or would give it a try. In truth, Caroline just wants someone to come along and save her. She can't believe her life has turned out the way it has—that she isn't married to a rich, successful, handsome man who takes her off to Europe and other faraway places. She is so angry she doesn't have what she thinks she should and stays so stuck in that place that all efforts to help seem to ultimately fail.

For Caroline, bringing in help, getting organized, and not being alone with her business also means letting go of getting attention by constantly complaining. I know it can be difficult to put the pieces together, to make all those arrangements, to go through each day planning, doing, setting things in motion. Most of us have a strong desire for attention and to connect to people so they will care. Only what happens in most cases is that constantly complaining and not solving an ongoing problem has the opposite effect. It turns people away, and Caroline feels more alone than ever. I doubt anyone will ever come along to save her. It could happen, of course. I just wouldn't hold my breath waiting.

Practically every entrepreneurial woman has to find her own way to balance her business and personal life. Taking care of business, taking care of oneself, and often taking care of others is constantly on our agendas. In fact, many entrepreneurial pioneers who have considered running away were really at the point where we weren't even allowed to cross the street yet.

For women whose work is strictly in the home, I am fully aware the home and hearth can be very exhausting and depleting. And when you are taking care of both business and home life, children or not, it's bound to have many moments that overwhelm and exhaust you.

Being overwhelmed and exhausted is really no laughing matter. However, sometimes we do need to laugh. For whatever reason, it helps keep us sane. We have to know absolutely that there is no way to do it all without some help.

I received a wonderful birthday card last year from one of my best friends. The card said, "You are one busy woman—always running, going, doing. And I imagine you're constantly being told that you need to slow down, take a break, not do so much. You're not going to hear that from me. I am amazed at your energy, inspired by your enthusiasm, in awe of your accomplishments. You are someone who is truly making a difference in the world. Instead of telling you to do less, I think we should learn from your example and each do a little bit more."

I love that card. I love my friend.

Also, I always ask for and expect good help!

THE SOLUTIONS

For much of the 20th century, women were financially dependent on men. The main recourse for getting what they needed was to behave in a consistently lovable, accommodating and pleasing manner. In fact, in the 19th century when women "disobeyed," many were thought to be mentally unbalanced and were placed in mental institutions. Traditionally, women have worked in the home raising children, cleaning, and tending to family and social life. Traditionally, women did not get help for themselves, did not seek to fulfill their dreams or ambitions, and in general were everyone else's helper and cheerleader. Today, as we enter the 21st century, hundreds of thousands of woman entrepreneurs are earning their own money. Yet, while they still spend the better part of their days engaged in business work, they often continue to accept more than their share of responsibility at home.

RoadBlocks for a woman entrepreneur that relate to being exhausted and overwhelmed include determining who's going to take care of the home life—especially if she's putting in many hours on her business, finding time to take care of her own needs, and getting good help at home and at work. These obstacles continually spur the common MindBlocks. Am I doing the right thing? Maybe I should be home. Can I really expect and receive good help and support? I can't quit early or take time off; I have too much to do. If I don't always say yes, people won't like me, and then....

It is all too common today for a woman entrepreneur to be exhausted and overwhelmed. Just ask a few you know. The expectations she places on herself and the expectations that others and society place on her can be demanding and eventually overwhelming. It's physically and emotionally unhealthy! It can lead to resentment, anger, and depression. For me it led enough times to physical illness for me to know I had better change my ways. I believe the only way a woman entrepreneur can "have it all" is to get some very good help and support, both in her work life and at home. You deserve it. You really *can't* do it all yourself. It *is* too much.

Solutions to stop being exhausted and overwhelmed fall into three categories:

- ▶ Assess and negotiate what you need and want.
- ▶ Get help—good help.
- ▶ Plan, prepare, and organize.

Assess and Negotiate What You Need and Want

Just Say No

- ▶ Learn to say NO. I can't do that for you. Practice saying NO. Stop working with people you can't say NO to. Why are their needs more important than yours?

- ▶ Regularly assess and negotiate what you need and want. What are the stress points? Are you succeeding in your business and enjoying your life? If not, what's getting in the way? (Get out that notebook or journal.)

▶ Be aware of which requests and demands make sense for you to accommodate and which ones take up time and energy that would be better spent elsewhere. Sometimes you could say no to a favor for a friend or relative when you can't afford to spend the time or—heaven forbid!—if you don't want to do it. Don't spend time with people who drain you of energy or put you down.

▶ Give some thought to which tasks you do. Just because women have traditionally done them doesn't mean someone else couldn't do them—someone you live with, someone you hire. I once hired a "househusband." He came to my home a couple days of week and ran all my errands, shopped, and helped with some research I needed for my business. It was great!

▶ Too often it's assumed that women will provide support tasks for free as part of their business. It would not be assumed if a man owned the business. You need to say a very polite, political "no" to some of those requests or charge enough to hire someone to do it. Leave yourself with the time and energy for what you know you do best.

▶ Women definitely have a certain mindset about seeking advice and input to get approval for what they are doing. Proper input and approval *is* important with clients and customers. Sometimes you need professional expertise and advice. But what makes other people who are not necessarily experts in a certain arena more right than you? In the interests of productivity and results, trust your own judgment. You're smart.

Fix or Eliminate Overly Draining Relationships

▶ Reassess your working relationships and eliminate the ones that drain you of your time, energy, and resources. Some people are just more trouble than they are worth. It could be a vendor, a client, an employee, or an associate. Practice saying, "You're fired." If you can't do it, bring in a business associate or advisor who can do it for you.

Don't Isolate Yourself

▶ Talk to someone you trust about issues like this.

▶ Start a women entrepreneurs' group to talk about issues like this that concern you. In the 1970s, women formed consciousness-raising groups whose focus was traditional social values and roles. It seems to me it's time for more consciousness-raising groups, with a new emphasis on women and business.

▶ Join professional organizations, networking groups; be around people who have similar needs, demands, lifestyles, and energies.

▶ Tell the people in your life how you feel. Pick a good time to have these conversations. Give them a chance to help and support you. You don't have to do everything yourself. You won't be rewarded in heaven—or anywhere else for that matter—for being a martyr!

Negotiate

▶ In order to negotiate effectively at your place of business or at home, you first need to know what you want, what you're willing to accept, what you'd ideally like to have. (That notebook or journal is calling you again.)

▶ Negotiate with people in your life. Yes, you should have more money. Yes, you should have more time. Yes, you should have more help. You need to ask for it and expect it.

▶ Negotiation is important business. Schedule time to prepare, time to negotiate, and time to follow through.

▶ Read a book on negotiating skills and use some of those techniques in negotiating with anyone in your life.

▶ Take a negotiation skills seminar and practice with a friend.

▶ Go to couples therapy with your partner, or find a mediator, so you can productively discuss and resolve issues about responsibility. It is more helpful when the other parties in your life can negotiate well, too. Learn negotiation skills together.

► Negotiate with *yourself* each day as to what will and what will not get done, making sure you leave time for yourself. Perhaps at the beginning of each week, make a list of things you would like to do just for you and what things absolutely must get done. Make some tradeoffs. What a wonderful idea! You get to do and have some things you really want just for you with a little self-negotiation!

Time Just for You

► Take some time each day just for you: taking a coffee break outside, having lunch with a friend, going on a date with your husband or boyfriend, going to the beach or movies, reading a book, writing in your journal, taking a walk, doing unhurried personal errands, shopping, enjoying music and candlelight in the evening, spending time at home doing whatever you please, buying some flowers, or whatever it is you enjoy or need. Plan ahead and schedule time in your appointment calendar. Whenever I go on a business trip, I take candles for the evening. It's soothing to me, and I love the atmosphere of lit candles. It's so important to take care of yourself.

Get Help

Make Help Affordable

► If money prevents you from getting the help you need, maybe you could barter time and services with some other business-women in your community. Check this out with some of the women you know from networking. Also call business organizations, nonprofits, churches, and schools for referrals for possible free services offered. Many businessmen are also willing to help as well.

► Get an intern from your local high school or college to help in the office.

► Consider your partner, your children, your mother-in-law, your great aunt, a friend, a neighbor for running errands, chauffeuring, helping with the home or business projects. Just tell the people in your life you need help.

► Look at your budget. Is there anything you could cut out or any way you can stretch dollars so that you could afford some help? Start slow: a half day or two half days a week for office help, someone to clean your home once every other week. When you free up some of your time from some of the mundane stuff that has to be done, you will make more money doing what you're supposed to be doing to grow your business.

Get Help at the Office

► Make a list of the kinds of help you need: bookkeeper, personal assistant, organizer, office manager, sales manager, clerk.

► For each category, make a list of people you could call for referrals. Call them and follow up on their leads. Ask someone who works for you to help make the calls if you don't have time or if it feels overwhelming.

► Place an ad in area papers and call local colleges to place on job boards. Be very specific about what you want. Set days and times to interview people. Hiring good people will free up your time so you can be more productive doing what you do best. If possible, ask someone to help you do interviews and select best candidates for you to interview.

► Make an announcement at any of your networking meetings.

Get Help at Home

► Do you need help with children? Investigate programs in your community. Read books, articles, and research about childcare and strategies for working parents. Ask other working parents what they do. Absolutely ask for referrals regarding good, very good, daycare available near you.

▶ Do you need help taking care of elderly parents or other relatives or friends? Senior citizen programs, senior daycare programs, meals on wheels, senior transportation, and more are commonly available in most communities. Do you need someone to help keep track of their health insurance claims and reimbursements? Would it help to hire an aide, someone to help with errands, shopping, yard work and repairs? Call these resources, ask them for referrals, and get help before you fall flat on your face!

▶ Make a list of what you do at home. How much time does it take you each week to do each thing? Maybe you could get other members of your family to do the same thing. Include cleaning, organizing, cooking, shopping, errands, gift buying, organizing social life, car care, home repairs, etc. Be sure to include childcare or look at those costs separately. Which things do you need help with more than others? You may want to read up again on negotiating skills. Perhaps you could agree to hire someone to do some things around the house or you could arrange to share more equally, if that's an issue. Take advantage of mail order and free delivery services. Ask other women entrepreneurs, friends, and relatives for more ideas. What has worked for them? *I always ask for and expect good help*.

Plan, Prepare, and Organize

When we begin to get exhausted and overwhelmed, one of the first things to suffer is our planning, prioritizing, and organizing.

▶ Build in some support systems to call upon. I have several good friends and my sons I can call when I'm ready to go over the edge. (Of course, sometimes they feel like pushing me!) I'm supposed to be smart enough to know when to take a break, slow down, catch my breath, eat right, etc. So are you!

▶ Think clearly and regularly about what help you need and when. What don't you like or want to do? Be prepared in advance for times when your business will be busy, when you might need extra help.

► Be sure you have a good planner or appointment book.

► Prioritize daily, weekly, and monthly.

► Keep a weekly priority list for your business; write down what you have to do and who you have to call. Make up a "to-do" and "to-call" form and have one for each week. Determine what you have to do and what you will ask others or staff to do. Plan ahead if you might need to hire someone for a special project.

► Schedule your appointments to give you time to do planning and organizing. Schedule these and your personal time into your appointment book so *your* needs don't get lost in the shuffle.

► There is an organization of professional organizers. A consultant can help you get and stay organized and can even do hands-on organizational work if you want.

► Do whatever is necessary to stay focused. Leave your answering machine on to take messages when you're very busy, working on deadline, or trying to concentrate. Let business associates and family know when you are unavailable and be firm about it.

► Give yourself permission to spend money on setting up your office and business in a way that's most efficient and effective for you. If you need a second phone line, a fax machine, a new filing cabinet, office supplies, get them. These are crucial to the success of your business.

► Organizing and planning are essential for your sanity! Don't live on the edge—you could fall off!

MY STORY

I had hepatitis twice many years ago. Drug-induced, it turned out, from an antibiotic. A therapist friend called me the second time and said, "You know you don't have to get sick to rest." I believe at some level I thought I did. I got sick to rest. I got sick to get attention. I was always so responsible. After all, who could do it better than me?

I was given the messages as a young child about being a responsible person. I once told a group I was speaking to that I felt as if I was the most responsible person I'd ever met. For everyone and everything else but me.

At the same time, I was determined to be a different woman than I saw my friends becoming. I wanted my own life, my own success, my own voice.

I also kept getting very tired.

It still happens at times. Only now people close to me know I make a real effort to take care of giving myself self-time. I've taken Fridays off for years. I ask for help and expect good help. I set boundaries around family and friends calling me during the workday. I value time to myself to feel centered and not pushed by the needs of a dozen and one projects or activities. I listen to my own voice that tells me when enough is enough or even on the verge of being too much. I let people who are involved with me personally and professionally know I can't do everything and I know that's just fine.

I don't need to be in control all the time. I don't need to be in the center of everything all the time. The better care I take of me, the better I can be for the people in my life I love and who love me, the better I can handle my professional responsibilities, the better person I am in general. I am actually hardly ever a lunatic anymore!

PARTING WORD

Beyond the MindBlocks and RoadBlocks that are causing you to feel exhausted and overwhelmed is a world of potential sanity. The problem is that when you feel exhausted and overwhelmed, it's hard to think clearly. It's difficult to believe you will ever get out of that mindset. I'm not adverse to a little bit of primal scream and crying, or perhaps some moments of escape. Then into action! Especially asking for help.

Session 3
Relationships

SESSION 3: RELATIONSHIPS

I'm Just a Girl Who Can't Say No!

It's How I Stay Loved, Connected, and in Control

Let's talk about your relationships with family, friends, business associates, staff, clients

In relationships of any kind, you need to know when to move beyond your history to help make the relationship work. Sometime you need to know when a relationship simply isn't going to work, even though there are really no bad people involved—just a bad situation. Sometimes good people are just not compatible.

Business relationships are no different from personal relationships. They demand attention, require give-and-take, cause conflicts that require resolutions, and have all kinds of moments. Some moments are good; others are tense and intense.

Women business owners have to negotiate effectively through their business relationships while at the same time dealing with personal ones. Family members and friends may not be supportive or they may expect more attention than you have the time, energy, or even the willingness to give. Children want you a lot, elderly parents want you even more, and you wonder when there will be time for you. In fact, when is it *your* time?

In the Wendy Wasserstein play, *The Heidi Chronicles,* she asks, "What do mothers teach their sons they don't teach their daughters?" I for one have taught my sons to respect women. They know how to do the laundry, cook, and even sew. I taught them there is a better way of being a man in the world than generations before taught their sons.

UNCOVERING THE SECRETS:
What's Really Bothering You About Your Relationships?

▶ Some of my relationships limit and hinder my success because of expectations and demands on my time and energy.

▶ I'm afraid of being abandoned. I don't want to be alone.

▶ It's my way of getting attention and some recognition.

▶ I'm afraid of losing business or giving business associates and clients cause to say bad things about me. Then I'll feel embarrassed.

What are your secrets?

THE SESSION

Building and Maintaining Good Client/Customer Relations

For some women, building and maintaining good client/customer relations is so natural and easy. For others it's difficult and tiresome. I have a friend who has owned her business for nearly 20 years. She loves talking with her clients, meeting with them, taking long working lunches. They know they can call her from early morning till early evening and even on weekends. If she's busy, they know she'll get back to them and share their concerns, discuss solutions, and plan strategies for moving forward with their work.

Cynthia says, "I love people. It fascinates me to know all about them, hear about what they're doing and their family and friends. I relish talking about the things happening in their lives. I enjoy all the elements of the social experience: conversation, good food, shared experience. I make sure I plan at least a couple of lunches or early evening meetings at restaurants with clients or business associates. It's really important to me and I find it very stimulating."

Cynthia and I have spoken many times about how to deal with clients: stay in touch with them, call back in a timely manner, follow up with work to be handled, let them know you value them. We both understand and respect the impact of our words and that different types of clients need to be treated with different styles.

We are also good friends, and I have had ample opportunity to observe her easy and remarkably generous nature. I, who have been in the public relations/marketing business for more than 20 years, do not like talking to clients on the phone for any length of time. They can definitely not call me at all hours. In fact, I often let my phone service answer even when I'm in the office. I'm uncomfortable with working lunches and, by the end of those lunches, I usually feel drained, claustrophobic, and ready for a walk in the park to clear my head. Mind you, I know it is not their fault. It is simply my needs and my style. I set meetings and times when I know I will be at my best and able to build and maintain these relationships.

I've dealt with clients who want me to call, check in, report, or update as needed and then say goodbye. I have others who want long, in-depth conversations and those lunches I dread. We all need to know that our language, our behavior, even our body language can make a good or bad impression. The successful entrepreneur knows how to read her clients and how to smile through gritted teeth when necessary.

I've been involved in many difficult client meetings, especially when I was doing work for major pharmaceutical companies and working with lots of "male suits." I had the choice of not working with them or working with them and their ground rules. They are demanding and difficult—and they pay very, very well. I was determined to find a way to make my meetings with them as pleasant as possible and my relationship with them work.

First of all, I refused to let them intimidate me. Second, I found out what their needs were in relation to working with me and, always, I was very prepared for each meeting, I provided comprehensive reports with copies for all in attendance and outlines of future activities, and I was willing to follow up in a timely manner on all reasonable requests. We worked together for a long time.

Ultimately, it is the client or customer who is paying your bills and keeping you in business, and they have a right to expect to be treated appropriately. But they do not have a right to be abusive to you, and there are indeed times some clients do not serve you or your business well and you have to part company. In fact, I have found that letting go of unpleasant or abusive business relationships almost always provides an opportunity for a better one to come into your life. By not feeling hassled, anxious, worried, or upset, you're able to bring in the quality of people you *should* be working with.

Cynthia told me, "I recently had a potential client on the phone. She was somewhat obnoxious in her attitude, and I could tell she would be very demanding. While I liked her concepts and even the potential for good additional income, I knew it would be a mistake for me to take her on as a client." The energy she would have spent dealing with this person would have truly taken away from her other work.

Sometimes it's difficult to say no when you need the money and you need the business. Each situation obviously has to be taken on its own merits and according to your own circumstances and needs. If you're going to take on a very difficult client, prepare to deal and cope with them. Having that plan can possibly make the difference in keeping you from wanting to kill them, your kids, or yourself!

"The customer is always right" does not necessarily always apply. However, it is a good place to start.

EXPECTING AND GETTING THE RIGHT HELP AND RESPECT FROM STAFF AND SUPPLIERS

Remember: you're the boss. You have every right to expect to be treated with respect.

One of my favorite stories that I have been telling for years is about a conversation I overheard at a party that involved one of

49

the owners of a very successful and well-known gourmet deli/ bakery on Broadway in New York City. He was explaining his philosophy of hiring and firing. Someone asked him during this conversation, "How is it you have such good employees? It's known they take great care of your customers and many of them work for you for what seems like forever."

"Simple," he replied. "Most employers usually know after two hours if a new employee is going to work out. I do. And I let them go immediately. However, most employers don't fire them for two years."

I've seen this time and time again. Women business owners in particular have a hard time firing an employee who should have long ago been sent to the unemployment line. It is part of our nature for many of us to be more patient, more understanding, more tolerant, and more caring. Thus, more easily taken advantage of in some situations. We need to be very careful of seductive relationships, even in business. This is about your livelihood and your future. Employees who are unable to live up to your needs and expectations and to your style of doing business should not be working for you. If you have hired someone you feel you just can't fire, then bring in someone who can help you do that.

> "I have to fire her," Brenda told me. "This just isn't working
> out. I'm not getting my needs met. I'm upset all the time. I've
> wanted it to work out so I have kept trying different things
> to motivate her. I've let myself get too friendly because I
> wanted to be a good boss and because I genuinely like her.
> Now it feels like an almost impossible situation."

> "Do you want me to meet with you and her and see if it
> can be salvaged?"
> "Yes."

After a couple of conversations about this employee, about whether she liked her job (she said she loved it), and watching how she was with clients and how she handled the work Brenda left for her do to, it didn't take a rocket scientist to see the problems. They were many.

Brenda's employee was not able to do the job she needed to do, nor was she willing to handle the clients the way Brenda wanted her to. She had become more of a liability than an asset. I told Brenda she had no choice. We had to fire her—and we did. It was very difficult, but we did. Because Brenda had asked for my help, she had the support she needed to do what was best for her and her business.

Your staff needs to adhere to your client/customer policies and to know that good client relations are essential to the success of your business. This is simply good business. While employees should be treated with the same respect as the employer wants, they are employees, and it is important to keep friendships outside of the business environment.

Sometimes it is difficult. When you put in long hours together, you're likely to develop a bond. But you need boundaries, a shared understanding of who is the boss and who is the employee. It is also difficult because we all need connections to other people, and it seems natural to develop relationships with people who come to work for you on a regular basis. You need to make those close connections in other ways—through family, friends outside of your business, networking activities, or other organizations.

When you become too personal and friendly with people who work for you, it's very difficult to tell them when you are unhappy with their work—and almost impossible for you to fire them. Brenda felt guilty and bad that she couldn't make it work out. She asked me what she had done wrong. Her only mistake was not firing her employee weeks before and that was because she had a friendly relationship with her and wanted it to work out. She let the difficult work situation go on longer than it should have—but not too much longer.

Because Brenda is very successful and very smart. She asked for help. I fired her employee.

I felt like The Terminator!

The same behavior applies to vendors and suppliers who work with you. If you are providing them with business, you have every right to expect them to treat you as a professional. It has been a challenge for women business owners to get male vendors or suppliers to take them seriously and to know they expect the same courteous and prompt treatment as their male customers. Vendors and suppliers need to meet your business requirements and follow through in doing what they say they will do.

Brenda has a good relationship with her vendors because she tells them what she needs, sets deadlines, and pays them well and on time. She expects them to take her and her business needs seriously and to respond to her in a timely and professional manner. She spends a lot of money with her vendors. So do many other businesswomen. Women entrepreneurs in the U.S. now gross in the TRILLIONS. They are making a significant contribution to the economy. We should be taken seriously. To ignore us would be foolish!

HAVING YOUR FAMILY AND FRIENDS ACCEPT AND RESPECT WHAT YOU DO AND WHEN YOU'RE BUSY

Getting Encouragement and Support

- ▶ How much are you willing to give up just to be accepted?
- ▶ Do your family or friends expect you to chat with them in the middle of a workday and seem annoyed when you say you're busy?
- ▶ Does your family think your husband should be making all the money and you shouldn't have to work?
- ▶ Does your husband or boyfriend want or even expect attention when you're on a deadline?
- ▶ Who encourages and supports who you are and what you do?

These are indeed the $64,000 questions.

Yet another one of my favorite points has been to tell women and men that one of the things I think is most important to me in a relationship with a man is that he thinks that who I am and what I do are as important as who he is and what he does.

Is this really asking for too much?

We women are tugged at by so many strings attached to our hearts, to our minds, and to our daily lives: our feelings and concerns for our parents, our husbands or boyfriends, other close relatives, friends, business contacts, their demands on us, their expectations of us.

> "I'm afraid my marriage is going to end in a divorce. My husband doesn't like when I work in the evening. But sometimes it's the only time I have. I spend my days with clients and taking care of our two-year-old. The money is important to us, and I like being in business. I like using my mind and my talents. It seems like not only does my husband get annoyed with me, but no one else in my family feels pleased about what I'm doing. I actually never get any encouragement. Mostly they want to know why I don't have time to go to lunch, or chat midday, or come over for a visit. They all seem to want to know what I'm trying to prove."

This is Jessica, and she has told me she feels so frustrated by not getting any encouragement or support.

> "How do I make them understand how important this is to me? I love what I do, and I think I'm pretty good at it. I don't want to give this up. I want to build a future for myself and share it with my husband and my daughter."

> "Have you told them how you feel? Have you sat down with them and said, 'I need your help?' Can you tell them, 'I need you to understand how important this is to me'?"

> "I don't know. I want to. I just think they want me to be what they want me to be. It makes them angry that I'm not as available for them as they would like. I think they're being selfish and self-centered because they are totally unconcerned about my dreams and ambitions. But I'm not to give up doing what I want and love."

Jessica and I talked at length about how to deal with this problem and what she was really afraid might happen. "I'm afraid my family will distance themselves from me, I'll be alone." These are her familiar connections, and few of us really want to distance ourselves from our families. We just want them to treat us nicely and be understanding and accepting of who we are and what we want to do with our lives.

"Of course I want their love. I just think it's unfair to expect me to give up all or part of my business. It's such a huge price. Most families don't expect that of their sons. Just because I'm a woman doesn't mean I shouldn't be able to put in the same efforts for my business success."

Unfair? Indeed. A reality in many families? Absolutely! It sadly reminded me of something my mom said to me one time:

"You're so smart, you could have really been somebody."

"Excuse me?"

"Well, we just didn't realize you were so smart."

"If I had been a boy, would you have insisted I become a doctor or lawyer or such?"

"Yes. We just thought a girl would get married and have children. Why did she need a career? When you started in business, your father and I thought it was crazy. What were you trying to prove?"

"Even now you're still mad at me."

"Yes, but you don't understand why."

"Yes, I do. You wanted me to marry someone who would buy me a big home with a two-car garage and you could brag to your friends."

"Yes!"

"Couldn't you be proud of what I've accomplished?"

"Well, yes, of course, but ...."

The "but" said it all.

How many women today are dealing with the "but"? "But you should do this and shouldn't do that." It takes a great deal of courage and fortitude to move beyond this type of history or family dynamics.

Women must bring into their lives friends and business associates who value who they are and what they do. They need to have relationships that acknowledge them and validate their decisions.

Jessica can only ask for acceptance and understanding. She certainly can't demand it. Jessica and I are still in the process of working on this dilemma for her. That she decided to bring me (or someone like me) into her life—to help her and to give her the encouragement she needs—was a big and important step.

One woman told me, "Women, I believe, are more intuitive. They read between the lines better and are more apt to determine hidden meaning in physical and verbal gestures." Another said, "I think our style is different from men's, but I don't think it comes from our biology. I think it comes from our history."

THE SOLUTIONS

These MindBlocks to success are understandable when one considers the RoadBlocks women entrepreneurs encounter that relate to their relationships. Though it is changing, men have long dominated the business world. A foundation for women's success and power has really been put in place only over the past 20 years.

Many women face problems and difficulties in both their business and personal relationships based on their needs and what is expected of them. Women have made significant and positive progress in changing the business culture, in setting up their relationships in ways that allow them to effectively pursue their business ambitions. But according to research conducted by the National Association of Women Business Owners, women entrepreneurs still need help with this issue. A recent survey reported that 38% of women business owners claim that the most significant challenge they face is *being taken seriously*.

Women business owners should be taken seriously. They are bringing over three trillion dollars a year into the U.S. Women have a right to be confident about their own styles and decisions and to become comfortable with success, wealth, and power if that's what they want.

Relationship solutions fall into four categories:

► Convey confidence and be comfortable with success.

► Build and maintain good business relations.

► Expect and get respect and the right help from employees and suppliers.

► Help your family and friends accept and respect what you do.

Convey Confidence and Be Comfortable with Success

Have Confidence in Your Style

According to 1994 research by the National Foundation for Women Business Owners, more than half of women business owners (53%) emphasize intuitive thinking or "right-brain" thinking. This style stresses creativity, sensitivity, and values-based decision making. Seven out of ten (71%) men business owners emphasize logical or "left-brain" thinking. This style stresses analysis, processing information methodically, and developing procedures. Women business owners' decision-making style is more "whole-brained" than that of their male counterparts, that is, more evenly distributed between right- and left-brain thinking.

Women entrepreneurs view their business relationships as a network. Men entrepreneurs focus more on set rules and procedures. Men are better able to delegate. Women are more perceptive and caring in their business relationships and able to balance different tasks and priorities. However, women and men entrepreneurs are more like each other than they are like the general population. Compared with the general working population, entrepreneurs are more logical and analytical in their decision-making.

Know what your style is and why it makes sense for your business. Have confidence in your own style. If your style is working for you, be comfortable with it.

I might work 80 hours some weeks, but for years I have always taken off Fridays, just for me. Rarely have I let someone talk me into meetings, appointments, or other business activities.

Expect to Be Taken Seriously

If you expect to be taken seriously, you must first take yourself seriously. If self-esteem is an issue for you, please refer to the *Self-Esteem Session* (Session 9).

▶ Write in your journal or notebook about the talents and skills you have. Add to it all the successes you've had, both business and personal.

▶ Express yourself with confidence. Be prepared for meetings and discussions regarding your type of business and area of expertise. It's important that you participate and allow yourself to be seen by having a positive presence.

▶ Prepare yourself with relevant facts, past successes, and credentials to persuade others.

▶ Don't oversell yourself. Don't speak so fast that others feel like they're being pressured. Sometimes saying less is more. I think entitlement is a good thing, but not arrogant entitlement.

▶ Whenever possible, eliminate people from your life who don't take your business interests and efforts seriously.

Build and Maintain Business Relations

Take Good Care of Business Relationships

▶ Don't take too much personally. Women are sensitive to people's personalities, expressions, and behaviors; it's what makes us good bosses and good friends. It becomes an interference when we react and sometimes overreact to others' expressions, behaviors, and comments in such a way that we then feel angry with ourselves, even diminished. It is all right to have a client or customer unhappy or upset—as long as you act to repair the problem. These things happen.

- ► Deal with any business problems as a professional. Identify the problems; consider the various solutions and options. Let the client or customer know you will take care of matters. If you need assistance, call people you know and ask for help. If you are overwhelmed, they don't need to know. You can scream after you've resolved the problem.

- ► Understand the objectives of the businesspeople you want relationships with and who you do work for so you can not only serve them well, but also be of value in networking and establishing strategic alliances.

- ► Plan get-togethers or other events and invite people who are important to your business—possibly just a wine, coffee, and dessert reception or you can make it fancier. Provide materials and information on your business for guests to take with them. Have some giveaways. My business associate gave away beach balls at a dessert and coffee reception in the Hamptons. Great idea!

- ► Make a plan or hire a professional to help you develop strategies for improving and maintaining good business relationships.

Stay in Communication

- ► Stay in contact with business associates and clients. Important business relationships need to be nurtured. Check in with them on a regular basis. Provide written reports and updates for service clients. Most clients have no idea how much work is involved in any given project. They appreciate knowing you are taking good care of them.

- ► Let clients and customers know when you have made progress on their behalf. Tell them when you've done something that can increase their business or save them money.

- ► Express to your clients and customers that you need their cooperation to be effective for them.

- ► Return calls promptly.

- ▶ Attend business networking meetings or events where you can have conversations in a non-business setting.

- ▶ Congratulate your clients/customers and other business relationships on their successes. Call them, send a card or gift, or take them out. Remember to send them and all your business associates holiday cards.

Expect and Get Respect and the Right Help from Employees and Suppliers

Be Clear About Expectations of Employees and Suppliers

- ▶ You don't need to be friends with your employees or suppliers. Pay them fairly and treat them with dignity.

- ▶ Be clear with your employees and suppliers right from the beginning about what you need and expect from them.

- ▶ Provide written descriptions of job responsibilities.

- ▶ Develop reasonable policies for your staff. Expect them to adhere to those policies.

- ▶ Employees need to know how you want the phone answered, how to deal with customers and clients, and what type of communication and public relations efforts will keep clients and customers coming back and referring others. Expect them to make you aware of a problem before it becomes a crisis. If things go wrong, it's your business on the line, not theirs.

- ▶ Employees need to respect that you're the boss.

- ▶ If an employee or supplier doesn't meet your expectations, speak with them about it.

- ▶ If an employee or supplier isn't serving you well, even after you speak with them, then fire them. Be sure you are legally protected. If concerned, talk to a lawyer.

- ▶ Hire new employees on a trial basis; it gives you and the new employee an opportunity to explore whether or not this is a mutually good business relationship.

▶ Hiring friends or family can be difficult and trying. In some cases it has the potential for disaster. If you do that, be sure you have ground rules in place. There are family business organizations across the country supporting family-owned businesses. You may have to be prepared to say, "I love you, but this is not working out."

Value Your Employees

▶ Employees appreciate being able to contribute in a meaningful way that uses their talents and thinking.

▶ If money is a problem, but you'd like to reward or motivate a good employee, consider another benefit, such as additional vacation, flexible scheduling, mentoring, training, or an inexpensive seminar. Consider bartering with another business for a product or service your employees might like.

▶ Say thank you at the end of the day. It's good for employees to leave feeling appreciated.

Help Your Family and Friends Accept and Respect What You Do

The support of family and friends is incredibly helpful for a woman entrepreneur. They can give you a sense of hope, courage, comfort, and acceptance. Tell them what it means to you to have their support and *how* they can support you.

Talk to family and friends about your business needs, concerns, and ambitions. Let them know you want them to be a part of your success.

Some family and friends simply will not accept, respect, or cope with you being busy and becoming a success. Sometimes you have to leave people behind. Sorry!

Some family and friends will be upset for a while, but then they'll get over it because they want you in their lives more than they want to be angry or upset.

Set business hours and tell family and friends they cannot call during those work hours except for an emergency. At the beginning or end of a workday, call to let them know you're thinking about them. Tell them that you care.

Share business news with them—good and bad. Let them be excited with you about the good and be supportive of you for the bad.

Don't let other people's voices hold you back. Remember: they are coming from their own fears and desires. You don't have to please everyone. Thank goodness!

MY STORY

Over the years I realized how familiar I was with discomfort and struggle. I often gave away my money and time, always for reasons I thought were very good. The problem was I couldn't say no. I knew I had to get over that or I would be running in circles forever.

It wasn't difficult to figure out I wanted everyone to think I was wonderful, I wanted everyone to love me lots, and I loved saving others. I forgot about me, taking care of me and saving me. We all need to do this. If we don't take good care of ourselves, how can we possibly continue to have the energy, the wherewithal to give others?

I'm not alone in this way of thinking. Believe me. I have spoken to many other women. I once did a survey with a group of women about why they behave in certain ways in business and why they let people get away with things they shouldn't. It almost always came back to the women telling me they how important it was for them to be liked or loved. Sometimes they wanted others to just think they were the best. Best *whatever*?

Business relationships can be just as demanding as personal ones. Business relationships are also often intertwined with our personal relationships—and all of this becomes so convoluted we absolutely have to step back and look at what we are doing and not doing. I certainly had to do that, not only in regard to taking charge of my own business and not letting male voices tell me their way was better, but also in regard to letting go of needing everyone I dealt with in business to love or like me and tell me how wonderful I am.

My worst time was when I became overly involved in donating time to numerous women's organizations. A good friend told me she thought I was addicted to giving to them, because I spent so much time going to their meetings and planning activities for them. I think she was right. I wanted other women to think I was terrific for what I was doing and how smart and capable I was for how much I accomplished.

I understand that we all need ways of being connected to other people. These connections need to be in ways that are healthier than giving away outrageous amounts of our time and money. We need to be connected by being equals, by being involved but within reason. We need to have a sense of balance in our business and personal lives and we have to bring people into our lives who value us, without trading our souls for their business, friendship, or love.

PARTING WORD

Trust your instincts. It's fine to be an understanding person; however, you don't have to tolerate inappropriate, unacceptable, abusive relationships.

Session 4
Sexism

SESSION 4: SEXISM

Men Intimidate Me

It's Still a Man's World

It's More Difficult for Women

Men Abuse and Harass Women

Let's talk about men and women

Do you know that women still earn only 74 cents to every dollar a man earns? And that's dropped recently from 78 cents. Do you know that some of the poorest people in this country are women over 65? Do you know there are very few women who are CEOs of *Fortune* 500 companies?

Why is there still a glass ceiling? Why are more women not in senior management and on major corporate boards? Women are still not treated equally in the corporate world or taken seriously in the business world. Yet, more and more women are quitting careers in the corporate world to start businesses of their own.

As an entrepreneur, a woman is in control of her own destiny. She doesn't have to depend on senior male management to promote her. She doesn't have to work twice as hard to prove she's equal to the task. Sexism in the work place is one of the strongest motivating factors for women to be their own bosses.

UNCOVERING THE SECRETS:
What Problems Do You Really Have Dealing with Men?

► They intimidate me.

- ▶ Because men have most of the money and power, they try to control relationships, including business ones. I don't know how to fight that and not lose my business.

- ▶ I think I'm smarter than a lot of the men I deal with in business, yet I find myself often trying to make them look smarter. It makes me really angry. I hide that anger.

- ▶ They don't take me seriously and I have to keep trying to prove myself and keep a smile on my face.

- ▶ I'm afraid of losing business.

- ▶ I'm afraid I won't know how to handle a situation and will react in a way that's harmful or embarrassing to me.

- ▶ What if I step outside of established roles?

Do you know *your* secrets?

THE SESSION

Dealing with Men in Business

The majority of CEOs of leading corporations are men. This includes banks, utility companies, publishing firms, advertising agencies, and the list goes on. They are also owners and sales reps of many of the companies that have become your suppliers. It has to be obvious to any woman in business the chances are you're going to have to deal with some men. They may be your banker, your landlord, your client, or your supplier.

How you deal with men in business is what's at issue here.

"They intimidate me, especially when we're in a meeting. I feel as if I have to constantly prove I have a right to be there, that I need to do more and better. I know sometimes this is just in my mind. Sometimes it isn't. It's as if they are waiting for me to mess up and show that they are the smarter, better ones. I know lots of women who feel this way. And while it's much better than it used to be, many of us believe we are not treated as equals."

All this is from Lisa, who has worked with men for years.

Lisa is right. She is not alone in how she feels. Many women still feel they are not treated fairly in the business world. One of the biggest issues for women that men rarely face is being taken seriously. "She doesn't really have to work. Her husband and her father have plenty of money. She's just doing it to keep busy." Baloney! Many women need the work. Many women want and need their own money.

Please know I do not think there is anything wrong with living with a wealthy person who wants to share with you, even possibly support you. We all make choices based on our own needs and wants.

Still, we are a society in which men seem to feel more entitled than most women do to having a lot of money, power, and business success. Women create their own angst by being too competitive with men, and sometimes they don't take credit for an idea or accomplishment, just so the men they're working with don't get upset over what they perceive as "being upstaged."

Financial success often becomes a compromise, both in personal and business relationships. I told Lisa I knew women who held themselves back in ways they couldn't even define until we spoke about it, because they felt that the more successful they were, the more disconnected they felt from people and in many of their relationships.

I know women who have let male clients take months to pay because they were uncomfortable calling and asking them for money, saying they didn't want to embarrass them or push them away. Others have let male vendors and suppliers get away with overcharging or with late deliveries because they didn't want to deal with confrontation.

It's difficult to be a success in business if you're unwilling to deal with confrontation or believe you have to be second to men in business situations. There is a wonderful article that appeared in the magazine *Insight* quite a few years ago, in which a speech by Barbra Streisand was quoted: "Language gives us an insight into the way women are viewed in a male-dominated society.

"For instance:

▶ A man is commanding; a woman is demanding.

▶ A man is forceful; a woman is pushy.

▶ A man is assertive; a woman is aggressive.

▶ He shows leadership; she's controlling.

▶ If a man wants to get it right, he's looked up to and respected. If a woman wants to get it right, she's difficult and impossible.

▶ Men and women are measured by a different yardstick and that makes me angry. Of course, being a woman I'm not supposed to be angry."

HANDLING SITUATIONS OF SEXISM AND HARASSMENT

He would ask me to call him at home on Saturday mornings. He said it was easier for him to discuss the projects I was working on for him. He said it was too hectic to talk during the day, during the week. The projects were in the fee range of six figures on a regular basis.

This was definitely a dilemma.

Fortunately he lived several hundred miles away.

"I would love to count your freckles." Oh boy, I knew this was going to be a big problem for me.

I know I had choices. I could simply walk away from the projects. I could tell him off in no uncertain terms. I could, of course, let him count my freckles. No, I think not!

I knew that I had to handle the situation and get rid of it. I had no doubt what very unacceptable and inappropriate behavior this was. I also wanted to determine if there was a way to diffuse the situation, keep the client, eliminate this type of behavior and the stress and upset it was causing me. He thought he was being rather cute and seductive. It was sexual harassment. He knew the account was very important to me, and he was the person who made sure I got the project.

I also knew he had a girlfriend. I decided I would open our conversations with "How is your girlfriend?" I got him involved in telling me his problems and joys, and it was almost impossible for him to move into the issue of me and my freckles.

I certainly do not mean to diminish the unpleasantness of the situation. Yet here I absolutely needed the work and the money it brought me, and I felt I at least wanted to make an effort to find a way to continue the business relationship if at all possible. If he had not responded positively and I could not deflect the situation, I would have resigned the account.

I can't tell anyone to do it the way I did. I had to look at my life, what I needed, and how I could establish this relationship in a way that eliminated that inappropriate behavior and kept me included in the business elements. Quite a juggling act.

For many women it is often a juggling act. We should look good, take good care of ourselves—but don't look too sexy. Our hair should shine, our nails should be buffed, and our makeup be flawless—but don't look too attractive. The truth is there's no reason for any man to harass or abuse a woman. None. End of story.

About seven or eight years ago, a business associate and I went to call on a potential client who owned a pharmacy in Westchester, New York. The owner made a very overt and unpleasant pass at me while my associate waited outside for me. He basically offered to give me his business if I was willing to give him whatever sexual favors he had in mind. He was very clear about that.

I was very clear about the fact that he was a slob and disgusting. I told him I was going to call the local newspaper and Chamber of Commerce. I did. Not that they printed my letter or acted on my complaint, but I sure felt better. I truly believe that today the paper and the Chamber would take complaints like this far more seriously. I think they would respond to them appropriately instead of dismissing them.

Women should not and need not keep quiet when they are being harassed or abused in any way. If it happened to me again, I now would also call his state and U.S. senators and representatives and an attorney and file a harassment complaint. And that's just to begin with.

There are many lawyers, law students, and supporters who have helped change the legal climate. They deserve our acknowledgment and appreciation.

UNDERSTANDING THE IMPACT OF TRADITIONAL SOCIAL AND FAMILY ROLES FOR WOMEN AND YOU AND YOUR BUSINESS

"More men have a background and foundation of income through family and savings," continued Lisa. "My own family was far more supportive of my brother than me. It took a lot more for me to get their support, and I felt like I had to prove myself over and over again even as my business was growing and becoming more and more successful."

Many men don't like the women in their lives to move beyond them. That means husbands, brothers, and even fathers. In fact, financial success can become a leveraging factor both at home and in business relationships. It can also be the cause of feeling disconnected in some relationships. It takes an effort and willingness on everyone's part to not let that happen.

Women are breaking new ground in business, finance, and their personal lives. They are asking for support from their families and learning to not be as emotionally or financially dependent. Sometimes when this does not happen in a family, women are seeking support from others and creating other types of bonds as strong as any good family. They are sharing and caring and helping each other.

There are people who just do not have the ability to grow and change and accept a woman on her own terms. They are unable because of their own limiting mindsets to support you, encourage you, be available for you. They are unable to let go of their own needs to see yours. They are unable to let go of their preconceived notions and attitudes about women.

"There are still a lot of double standards existing. For instance, my husband expects me to make as much money as he does and until I do my efforts are 'playing.' However, he received complete schooling and I had babies. He started his career when he was 28; I started my career when I was 45 and, at age 57, I still have a teenager at home who needs me."

Marilyn is facing some of the difficulties and disadvantages of starting a business a little later in life. She's also discovering some of the male mindset.

"Men have permission to spend more time at work when they need to in order to be competitive. Many women have to be home for their families, even when their business needs additional attention. I also believe if a male is speaking with a male, they understand each other and believe each other. If a female is speaking with a male, the male reads into it and thinks she means something different from what she is saying. It's difficult. I think our style is different from men's, but I don't think it comes from our biology. I think it comes from our history."

I told her I absolutely agree! And to keep in mind there are times some women can be problematic for other women. Issues of race, class, and lifestyle can present great barriers. Still, while sometimes offensive and unpleasant, it does not usually have the somewhat universal impact of sexism.

Jenny also experienced sexism in business. She was co-owner and equal partners of a business with three men and she says, "I'll never, ever do that again." When she went to apply for a credit card for the company, she had a difficult time being approved; for some reason they thought she was a hooker.

"It was just always difficult; they had their own agenda and it was different from mine. They felt a woman should only do certain things and the rest should be left to the men."

I've heard so many of these stories over the years. It's better than it used to be, yet we still have miles to go. Women who have owned their own businesses for many years tell me, "Some men still don't take me seriously, the old boys won't let me into their club, there are few female role models, men certainly don't like me being in control, and it's still difficult to find funding for a woman-owned business."

THE SOLUTIONS

Remember, it was only in 1890 that wives won the right to keep their own paychecks, and it was only in 1917 that women won the right to vote! It always amazes me that women were *ever* in such a position of having little if any financial freedom and no direct political power.

Still, no matter that Freud didn't know what women wanted, women did what they had to do. They worked in the factories in the 1940s to make up for the shortage of men who went to fight in World War II. Women went back in the home after the war.

A quiet revolution for women's rights began to grow in the '50s and '60s, and by the '70s women were shouting for all to hear what it was they wanted. Equal rights! Equal pay! The women's movement—including the consciousness-raising of the '70s—brought out the truths of what women were feeling, and they began to open new doors of opportunity for themselves. By the 1980s more and more women became professionals, got jobs in corporations, and said they wanted a turn at doing more than taking care of other people. They wanted to fulfill their own dreams and ambitions. Literally thousands opened businesses of their own.

Becoming an entrepreneur was the answer for many of the women who found they'd hit a "glass ceiling" at middle and upper management of corporations. They wanted an opportunity to utilize their talents, have a place that valued and gave infinite opportunity to their ambitions, and offered flexible hours for those doing parenting. Huge numbers of women left corporate America.

Sexism was and continues to be alive and well even for women entrepreneurs: unfair lending practices by financial institutions, relatively few government contracts, lack of support at home, and constant comments and treatment reminding women they face greater challenges to success than their male counterparts. Absolutely true!

Thankfully, a lot has changed over the past 20 years in terms of RoadBlocks. Yet, the impact of sexism has definitely caused Mind-Blocks. Feelings of anxiety, intimidation, and even fear exist in certain business situations involving interactions with men. Some women cover up how smart they are so men won't feel threatened. Others feel the need to constantly go above and beyond to prove themselves so they will be accepted and taken seriously.

We've made progress in reducing the RoadBlocks of sexism. Equally important is how you can overcome the related Mind-Blocks. Hopefully we will find ways to change this sooner rather than later. We're working on it!

Solutions to the MindBlocks and the RoadBlocks to success related to sexism lie in three categories:

▶ Dealing with female/male relationships in business.

▶ Expect to be taken seriously by men.

▶ Know that women have as much right to success as men.

Dealing with Female/Male Relationships in Business

Win with Men

▶ So, do you feel intimidated by men? Your personal history can probably provide clues to why certain situations make you feel uncomfortable. Are you so angry about sexism it affects your attitude and ability to do business with men? Acting out of anger in business is counterproductive.

▶ Learn how to deal with confrontation, conflict, negotiation, and money. These are issues that men are familiar and comfortable with. If you are in a business that requires frequent dealings with men, it will benefit you to understand their language and way of doing business. It is usually more straightforward and to the point. I'm not saying you have to do it their way; just understand it and know how to maneuver around it. It can be helpful to rehearse a conversation for a specific situation with a business associate or friend. If you have to make a call to someone and you think there might be some conflict or confrontation, write yourself a script or list of points you want to be sure to cover during the conversation. If you are concerned about going to a difficult negotiation or where there might be conflict, ask a business associate to join you. Think about what your needs might be for any meeting or situation and plan ahead. BE PREPARED!

▶ Trust yourself, your strengths, and your abilities. When dealing with men in business, know you're just as smart and just as capable. You have as much right to be in business as anyone else. Talk to a business associate or trusted friend before going to a meeting with someone who you know behaves inappropriately. Vent your upsets and frustrations. Getting it out will ease your angst and probably give you some insights on how to deal with the situation.

▶ If you want or need to continue a business relationship with someone who makes sexist comments or otherwise behaves badly, then be prepared to know what you need to do to win with this type of person—more than just being right. What outcome do you want? You can try telling him how much you appreciate doing business with him but his comments make you feel most uncomfortable. *You most likely can't change him.* You can change your responses. You can absolutely move beyond any of his comments. Don't feed into them; ignore them. He's a jerk! Another tactic: you can bring someone to the meetings with you.

▶ You absolutely have to maintain some sense of humor, and sometimes you will find it helpful to use that humor to defuse an uncomfortable or unpleasant situation. I use humor a lot. I can often get my point across quite clearly with some gentle humor and funny comments.

- If the sexist comments or behavior turn into harassment, talk to a woman attorney and discuss your options.

- There is an enormous and talented women's market out there for you to tap into if it's too uncomfortable for you to work with men.

- Know that there are good men in the world.

Expect to Be Taken Seriously by Men in Business

Be Powerful

- You know the phrase, "act as if." Well, if you "act as if" men take you seriously, you will begin to see that many of them will do so.

- Focus on getting results and building relationships that help you get results.

- Be involved with people and organizations where you can demonstrate your abilities and create opportunities for yourself.

- Treat clients and business associates to lunch or such.

- Be as generous as possible. Philanthropy is a great source of building power relationships. If you can't afford to donate money, donate your time, your services, your product. Gain respect and recognition in your community.

- Serve on boards for business or nonprofit organizations. It is another excellent opportunity to develop strong business relationships.

- You can be angry. You have the right to be angry if you want. Just don't act out of anger; it rarely serves you well.

Be Professional

- For your sake, you want to eliminate any opportunities for sexist comments. Don't give the bad guys a chance to do say something stupid!

▶ It's OK if you have to take care of something unrelated to business during business hours. Having the freedom and flexibility to accommodate your lifestyle is an important reason why so many women go into business for themselves. However, it may be best not to discuss the real reasons for your absence with business associates, even your employees. "I have an appointment" or "I will be unavailable" is sufficient and sounds professional.

▶ Be sure your phone is being answered professionally, whether by a person or machine.

▶ Keep appointments, be prepared, and please be on time.

▶ Sorry, but you do need to dress the part. That also, of course, depends on the type of business you have and its locale. I definitely dress up more for business when I meet clients in New York City than when I'm at my place of business in Westhampton. Different lifestyle, different needs. But I always dress with respect to the image I want to have.

▶ Keep emotional behavior out of your business relationships. You can cry, yell, rant and rave by yourself or to other people in your life.

Know That Women Have as Much Right to Success as Men

▶ Develop relationships that support who you are, what you want to do and hope to accomplish.

▶ Stop listening to the voices—external and internal—that want to stop you.

▶ You have to know which fights are worth engaging in and which ones are not worth your time or effort. A lot of sexism is worth the fight; I've been there. Some of it is not worth it to you and your business. You can't afford to hold onto the anger if you want to be a success.

► Create an environment for yourself that feeds your ambitions and your dreams and nurtures your soul. You have a right to your own style of doing business and your own success.

MY STORY

I never understood, or accepted, that women could not be as accomplished as men. It never made sense to me. I once asked a rabbi, "Are you saying because I'm a human being in a woman's body, I can't participate in certain things that a man can?" He of course gave me some interesting interpretation of mystical writings. It didn't change at all how I felt. Or still feel.

Instinctively I knew being in business was better for me than working for anyone else with his or her rules and expectations of a woman's place.

The one full-time job I had for about a year as head of promotions for a television station just fueled the fires of my resolve. I discovered that because of being a woman I received a third less pay for the same job a man (and an incompetent one at that!) had been doing before me. I spoke with my boss, whom I had always considered a good man and good to me, and asked him what this was all about. He told me, "He has a family to take care of." In fact, so did I. That was that: he did not give me more money.

I began preparing for my public relations business right then and there. I knew I could not allow myself to be in that situation for long. I really hated it! I'm just better as an entrepreneur than as an employee. I like the flexibility, the opportunity to use my talents and abilities for my own gain and to be in charge. I definitely like being in charge of my life and my destiny.

Whether in business or personal life, the years of struggling to be given the same consideration and taken as seriously as the men I dealt with have given me an incredible determination to succeed and to be treated fairly.

I have been behind the scenes in the fight for women to be treated as equals and paid as equals. I have supported women running for office whenever possible and when I believed they were the best candidates. I have sat on the boards of numerous women's organizations, donating endless hours, especially in regard to economic development issues and related conferences. And I began to write and speak out—to talk to women, to tell women they must have economic independence.

It feels as if it's been a battle where the other side has had major weapons of destruction—control of finances, corporate leadership, political and financial power, physical and emotional abuse, and the determination to withhold opportunities. But on our side we have had our own determination plus awareness, talent, and vision. We now have successful women in important positions in business and the corporate world supporting our efforts for continued achievement by investing their intelligence, power, and money.

We have proven we make significant contributions to the U.S. economy. We expect to be taken seriously and treated with dignity. We are continuing to make our presence felt as we take on leadership in all areas of our lives. Don't fool with us. We mean business!

PARTING WORD

Be a success. It's the best revenge for sexism!

Session 5
5
Fears and
Anxiety
Attacks

SESSION 5: FEARS AND ANXIETY ATTACKS

I'm Afraid if I Do, I'm Afraid if I Don't

I Was Taught I Should, I Was Taught I Shouldn't

Let's talk about your state of mind

I n the early part of the 20th century, Freud asked, "What do women really want?" The question he should have asked is "What are women really afraid of?"

A century later, even though we have had the "audacity" to expect to be treated with respect and dignity, be valued for our abilities, and of all things, be taken seriously, the truth is we are still afraid of verbal, emotional, and physical attacks. We are constantly fearful of being hurt and having our livelihood threatened.

Just look at the list of symptoms women have exhibited to me over the years. We are afraid of the consequences of our responses and actions, and these fears cause us to act and not act in certain ways. Long before we were born, our histories formed our roles in society and in our families, and in no place is this more evident than the business world.

UNCOVERING THE SECRETS:
What Is It That Really Makes You Frightened and Anxious?

- ► I'm afraid of being a failure, of possible bankruptcy.
- ► I'm afraid of losing my temper, losing my clients.
- ► I'm afraid of being yelled at or criticized in front of others. It makes me feel ill.
- ► I'm afraid of my marriage failing. What if I can't take care of myself financially if I'm divorced?

▶ I'm afraid my children will hate me for working so much.

What are *your* secrets?

THE SESSION

Fear of Failure

Diana told me she has wanted to start her own consulting business for a long time. "I'm so afraid of failing. What if I can't do it? What would I do if I failed?" These and questions and comments like these so often mask the real fears. "What if I lose all the money I have? What if I have to work 20 hours a day, seven days a week to make this business a success?"

I asked Diana what was bothering her most.

"What are you really afraid of? You have wanted to start this business for such a long time. You've had a good-paying job for years. You could start this consulting part time. Let's design a business card and some stationery, maybe even a simple brochure that identifies what it is you do. We'll decide where you should distribute it, to whom you should give it, who might be interested in your consulting services. It will provide you with an opportunity to see if you get some response and how you work with these people."

We discussed how to set up an office in her home and the equipment and supplies she would need to do the consulting. We developed interview forms, follow-up forms, and other communication materials.

"I feel better, but I'm still scared. What if I can't give them what they want? How will I know if I'm doing a good job?"

You have to trust what you know. You have to be connected to all the successes you have had in your career. When your clients talk to you, listen to what they are saying, pay attention to their concerns and their needs. Give them time to talk to you, and when you respond, let them know by what you say that you heard them. Give them suggestions that relate to their needs. If you don't have an immediate answer, let them know you want to think about what would be best for that particular situation and that you will get back to them within a day or two with some ideas. If they want a proposal, be fair to yourself in accepting that it might take a few days or a week. There are enough pressures without making yourself crazy by pushing your sensible and reasonable time frame for providing information and materials. You'll do a better job. All clients push. Gently say, "I can get this to you by Thursday; Tuesday is just too soon for me to do that for you." You get the idea.

You'll know you're doing a good job because you'll probably keep them as a client. They might be thoughtful enough to compliment your work, and they might even refer you to other clients. You'll know. If you're not doing a good job, they will let you know, by telling you, asking you to rework something, or firing you. Simple.

Understandably, Diana was nervous, but at heart she had the courage to move beyond her angst. She asked for help. She talked about her concerns. She developed strategies for starting and growing her business and for joining networking groups. She was determined not to let momentary upsets interfere with her dreams and ambitions.

Judith's problems are a different story. She had spent her entire work experience working for someone else. She found becoming an entrepreneur an overwhelming transition. An article in *The Wall Street Journal,* "Hear Them Roar," stated, "More and more women are quitting lucrative careers to start their own businesses. Women plunge into being entrepreneurs and there is a whole set of new problems."

How true that is. Suddenly they do not have a regular paycheck. They are the boss and responsible for all the decisions, getting the new business, and finances. And that's just part of it. There is the management, dealing with crises, and being chief cook and bottle washer.

"I know I'm good at what I do. I've been working with people for years in my job, helping them through difficult situations. I'm actually afraid that I'll just be concentrating on being afraid. I know that sounds absurd, but I keep thinking about being afraid and why in the world am I putting myself through all this? How do I step away from it and give myself a chance? I really believe I can do this; it's just all those voices, internal and external, telling me what to do and not to do."

We discussed the possibility of some therapy to deal with her real fear issues and how to listen to her own voice. Perhaps it would help her not to listen to the negative voices in her life or the internal voices that came from generations in her family taking away permission from her desire to be a successful businesswoman.

I told her a business consultant I worked with once told me, "When you're not worrying about money, you're making plenty of money." How true! When I was frightened about earning enough money, having enough clients, paying the bills, I would be so focused on all of those issues that it was nearly impossible to bring the right energy or time to taking care of my business and my clients.

Funny, quite some time ago I asked a rabbi friend of mine what he thought was the most important thing one needed to be successful. He said, "You first." Of course, he's a rabbi. What else could I expect?

"Taking action," I responded, "sometimes even massive action. Now you."

"Faith," he replied. We looked at each other and quietly and absolutely agreed. It was both. You need to take action and you need to have faith. It makes me smile when I think about it because over and over I have found out how true it is.

Judith was taking action as she moved into her consulting business. She needed to take other actions that related to her constant fears. Now she needed belief and confidence as well as faith in her abilities and in the process it takes to build a successful business. Sometimes when she gets frightened about business, she calls. We talk about what she needs to do right then and there to know she is doing well and that she does not have to be attached to some old beliefs about women and business—that women do not belong in business, that business is a man's world. These are old beliefs that can hold women back and keep us from being all we are capable of being.

Diana's fears decreased when I provided her with good information and resources. Everything was new to her, and once she spent the time gathering the right information and talking about her transition, she become stronger and more confident. Our work together likewise helped Judith with her fears. However, because she still carries the burden of so many years of being told who she could and could not be, she will need to be connected to reassuring resources for a long time. She can still be a success. It might just take a little longer.

Fear of Rejection and Ridicule

Kathy: "I can't. I just can't. I know I should make a presentation at those meetings, but I am terrified of saying something foolish or forgetting what I wanted to say."

Patricia: "I wanted to tell my client their idea was stupid. I know there is a nice way to do that, of course. I just was so afraid they would get upset with me for not agreeing with them. They might have fired me. Or worse, they might have yelled at me."

I have a good friend who said I ask these Socratic questions to get to the truth when I am talking with businesswomen. I ask, "What are you really afraid of? What do you think would happen to you if you made a mistake when you're speaking? What would happen if someone yelled at you?"

Unpleasant. Uncomfortable. Unacceptable. Perhaps. For most of the dozens and dozens of women I've met with and spoken to, including Kathy and Patricia, the fears are so much a part of how they were raised and of what was expected and not expected of women. After all, many of us were told as children, "You should be seen, but not heard." "It's not a woman's place." "Why do you need the money? A man needs to earn it for his family more than you do."

My intention when I respond to these comments is to provide insights into the fears, sometimes suggest good therapy, and always offer practical solutions.

Kathy can get help writing and preparing for her presentation. She can rehearse until she is at least somewhat comfortable and familiar with what she's going to say. She can have notes and, when she speaks, say she is going to refer to her notes because she has some very good information to present and she does not want to leave anything out they will find valuable. She can arrange to call or meet a friend immediately after the meeting or later that day to check in, calm down, and get centered, a friend to applaud her for making her voice and message heard.

Patricia has to find a way not to take it personally. This is business. And while she might continue to feel uncomfortable, the more she understands and accepts that this isn't personal, the more relaxed and real she will be.

I have worked with clients who yell and intimidate. I told one halfway through a meeting that if he didn't like my work I could leave now. He acted shocked. I stopped him in his act of being obnoxious when he saw I wasn't going to stand for him acting like a bully.

Women have to stand up for themselves and often we need the support and advice of others to assure us we have the right to do such things.

Using Your Vulnerability to Protect Yourself

We all know and have been told, "There is a time and place for everything." Nowhere is that more true than in the business world.

Crying is a no-no. Temper tantrums are unacceptable. I was very upset when a major female political figure cried on national television. I felt betrayed. How are we supposed to show how tough we are if we weep so easily? The problem is that our own image is so often taken as the reality.

We women have human fears and anxieties. Yet the business world needs us to appear strong and together. We tried for quite some time to follow the male model of being in business and have now determined it is not going to be business as usual. No more only the male hierarchy, the competitive "war" mentality. Women are seeking to problem-solve in business with a different style of strength and with dignity for employees and for ourselves. We care about childcare and eldercare; we are more communicative and less authoritarian. We are creating a business environment that is like a web, reaching out and connecting, while learning to keep our power and position for ourselves.

Quite some time ago, I was in a meeting with a woman business associate and 15 or 16 professional men. My associate made a comment about the money they owed us. One of the men became loud and verbally abusive. Talk about a war mentality and behavior. Attack! She sat there stunned. I, being a bit older than she, commented that his behavior was not necessary and the meeting moved along. My associate was fantastic. She held herself together until we left. Then she let it rip. She was furious, angry, and ready to storm this group of men with a hose. We calmed down and talked about how to handle the situation. She called the man who had behaved so badly and told him she would not accept treatment like that and was ready to resign. She knew he did not want her to resign. He loved her work. He apologized and said he knew he behaved badly.

What's interesting was that from that day on they had a much better working relationship. I know it's because she didn't let him get away with it, yet she reacted like a professional in the meeting when in truth she wanted to get up right then and there and tell him to . . . , well, you know what!

The problem is that feeling threatened in situations makes us feel vulnerable. Once that vulnerability takes over, it is difficult to feel and act powerful. The worst thing to do is hold it inside. When someone makes you feel vulnerable in your business life, it is important to talk about it with someone whose opinion you value and trust. It might be a business consultant or business associate, sometimes even a trusted member of your staff, or maybe someone in your family who respects you and your work. Don't hold it inside. It can only damage your motivation and your resolve to succeed. Use your vulnerability to protect yourself, but don't let it become an emotional issue that makes you feel impotent and powerless. This is a good time to trust your female strengths and know you can be vulnerable without acting weak, you can be frightened without quitting.

THE SOLUTIONS

Being a woman entrepreneur takes a great deal of courage. I believe women entrepreneurs are great heroes for having the courage to start and grow businesses of their own. It's amazing the absolute tenacity and persistence they're able to find within themselves. Women entrepreneurs often have so much stress based on the numerous and varied issues they have to deal with. Too much fear and anxiety, especially over a long period of time, is destructive and harmful to your business and your personal well-being.

Here are some common fears businesswomen have and ways to reduce and eliminate them:

- ► Fear of failure
- ► Fear of rejection and ridicule
- ► Fear of success

Fear of Failure

Take It One Step at a Time

- ► Think of your business success as a process, not as something that will happen overnight. Make a monthly plan, a weekly action plan, and a daily action plan. Take it one step at a time.
- ► Resolving inner conflicts that keep you from taking action can help you to reduce or eliminate the fears. You may need the help of a therapist to explore what's really behind your fears.

▶ You can't do it all alone. You need help. If you're exhausted and overwhelmed trying to do it all, see *Session 2: Exhausted and Overwhelmed!*

▶ Stay in frequent communication with people you speak with about your fear; know you have a network of people who support you and believe in you. When you're having a bad moment, make a call to someone who would understand.

▶ When something goes wrong—a client is upset, your finances are in bad shape, there's a dispute with a customer—and you feel like you're going to fail, get support from someone to help you move past the upset. Then take the necessary action. Don't let the fear paralyze you.

▶ If you feel discomfort with networking, go with a business friend. Having someone to "hang out" with helps a lot. Promise each other you will introduce yourselves to a least five new people. You'll give them your card and ask for theirs. A lot of being willing to network and make follow-up calls has to do with both time and self-esteem. As for time, you have to create the time; it's about building your business. As for self-esteem, well, we're working on that later on in the book!

▶ If you're terrified at the thought of having to introduce yourself at a meeting, you are among the thousands who feel great panic in any type of public speaking. Practice what you will say. Practice what you want to say in one or two sentences. "My name is _____ and I own a widget business based in _____." Practice alone; practice with others. Write it down, rehearse it, and memorize it. Go to meetings where there are small groups of people. Practice with them. Then move on to bigger crowds. You could also benefit from taking public speaking courses or joining a local Toastmasters group to develop speaking skills.

Fear of Rejection and Ridicule

Be Well Prepared

▶ Be sure you are well informed, know your facts, and prepare thoroughly for your business needs, business meetings, and business growth.

▶ Rehearse meeting presentations and speeches. You'll feel less anxious and perform better.

▶ Ask a friend to take the other side and prepare for every point that could be raised against you. Eleanor Roosevelt suggested this long ago.

Handle Rejection and Unpleasant Situations

▶ Don't confuse rejection of your *product or service* with rejection of *you*. Usually the person is actually rejecting the idea of spending his or her money.

▶ Your ideas may not always be accepted or applauded. Don't let it keep you from trying new things or expressing yourself.

▶ If you're afraid of being ridiculed or treated in some other way that makes you feel diminished by men *or women*, be prepared with a few well-chosen comments. You can usually disarm unpleasantness by calmly expressing your displeasure. Sometimes you may just have to excuse yourself in order to protect yourself.

▶ Get professional help if you let men intimidate you in business situations. Chances are you have to deal with men in your business. Don't ignore this until you are so stressed you decide to spend your life chanting in airports.

Fear of Success

Fear of the Consequences of Success

The time a woman entrepreneur devotes to her business may be time away from her children.

► Be *honest* about your needs and your children's needs. (I know you're concerned that if you're not around all the time they will grow up to be mass murderers!)

► Let your children know in some way everyday you love them. That's what they need most.

► Know what kinds of childcare services are available. What is affordable? What is convenient?

► Ask for referrals from other business mothers in your community and business groups. Get help making good choices and decisions.

► Talk to other successful women entrepreneurs with children. Ask them how they balance their business and family time.

► Put time aside for your relationships, no matter how busy or successful you get. Make dates.

► Share your concerns, hopes, successes, and failures with your partner. Keep him a part of your whole life.

► When you're successful, be generous with the people you love and care about. (I don't mean to let them take advantage of you!)

► Help people in your life understand that part of what you're doing is to help provide for what they need and want.

► Talk to successful women entrepreneurs about your concerns. See what they have thought and done.

Fear of the Unknown
Business success for women is only beginning to thrive. We have relatively few role models.

► Envision success and what it could be for you.

► Remind yourself of any and all past successes—even if they were in grade school.

► Talk to successful women entrepreneurs about their experiences. Join a women's business organization and ask some successful women entrepreneurs to spend a little time with you discussing your questions and concerns.

Reducing and Eliminating Fears

▶ Identify what you're really afraid of: lack of money, relationships, too much responsibility.

▶ You absolutely have to talk with someone about how you feel—a friend, a business associate, other women entrepreneurs. Venting helps a lot. So does asking for help. *It's OK to ask for help!*

▶ Take an honest look at your business situation and determine where you really need help, advice, support, information, contacts, money. Once you know, reach out as soon as possible to someone who you can rely on for good advice or for a referral to someone who can help you with your business concerns.

▶ Honest, from years of experience I can tell you that eating right, exercising, and avoiding sugar can help you be more calm and thus deal more effectively with your fears. (Notice I'm not telling you to give up your morning coffee.)

MY STORY

I was 13 years old and quite a brat. I was also an only child and, I know, very much loved. I had an argument with my dad for some reason or other I can't begin to recall. I insulted him, and I have no doubt I hurt his feelings. He responded by refusing to talk to me until I apologized. I refused to apologize for what seemed like a long time. I was more than just a little stubborn. I guess he wanted to teach me an important life lesson.

This incident had a profound impact on my life. To this day I am uncomfortable with direct confrontation. Now, however, I know when I need to protect myself and how I need to avoid escalating disagreements. Most of the people in my life are not argumentative, except (believe it or not) for one of my best friends. I just ignore when she gets argumentative. I can't be pushed into word wars.

In business I recognize the signs of argumentative people: they are defensive, eager to disagree, and more concerned with being right than doing what's right. Argumentative people do not work for me. They are not my vendors. When I have clients who are very argumentative, they are no longer my clients.

Who needs that aggravation? Disagreements, intense conversations, and a difference of opinion on ideas is a natural part of being in business, but overly argumentative situations are not necessary and, at least for me, have no place in my life. So there!

I have, however, found a way beyond one of my earlier and great fears. Like thousands of others, I had a fear about public speaking that gave me heart tremors, made my eyes glaze over, and caused my mind to go blank the first few seconds after I stood up to speak. The worst was I was sure everyone could notice my mouth looking like I had some serious nervous disorder. What made this such a huge problem for me was that I really loved and wanted to be a public speaker.

What to do?

I decided this was definitely a MindBlock I needed to move beyond. Whenever I thought about my fear of public speaking, I recalled being on stage in a grammar school play and forgetting my lines. I couldn't have been more than eight. I remember feeling very smug I had my lines all memorized. But suddenly I forgot some of them. I felt so embarrassed and almost humiliated.

I knew that my reaction as an adult was getting in the way of my doing something important to me. I just knew I could become a good public speaker. It became a mission for me to be one.

I was willing to spend money on something I wanted just for me. I joined Toastmasters, I took private lessons, I took a full-day workshop, I read books, I practiced, I had help writing speeches, and I listened to my own voice. I had good information about being a success in business and I had the ability to motivate and encourage others. At first it was good for me to promote my business through speaking engagements and, later, I knew it was important as part of my work with women.

Now you can't keep me quiet. I love public speaking. I am totally comfortable with it and believe it's because I am prepared, I have trained, and I have taken the time to do what was needed to move beyond what was indeed a stumbling block for me.

There was a period of a couple years, quite some time ago, when I would accept speaking engagements and then cancel a couple of days before with some nonsense excuse or other. Not great for the reputation! I apologize to the members of those groups, wherever you are.

We all have had experiences in our lives that set us up to react and behave in certain ways in our relationships with others. Understanding what they are and putting them in a perspective that allows us to move beyond them is so essential to living without fear and with hope, happiness, and accomplishment.

We each need to reach a place in our lives that allows us to know we can't change our history. We can only value our lessons and be our best selves right now.

PARTING WORD

Have some fun with your friends, your family. Hug your pet. Get a hobby. Sit in the park. Meditate. Give yourself a break!

Session 6
The Great Pretender

SESSION 6: THE GREAT PRETENDER

I'm Always Faking It: the Orgasm Syndrome

Let's talk about what you fake
and how you fake it

Why do women give away their power? In little ways and bigger ones, they often give away their dreams and hopes. We pretend to be coy and cute when we are really tough and smart. We pretend to be easygoing and understanding when we are really determined and demanding.

Men love their power; women should too. We don't need to be afraid of what we know—or even what we don't know. We don't need to pretend; it is so limiting and so hurtful to ourselves.

UNCOVERING THE SECRETS:
What Is There About You That You Don't Want Anyone to Know? Why?

► I pretend I don't know certain things so I can get others to feel sorry for me and help me.

► I can act really arrogant or quite charming when, in fact, I'm terrified someone will discover I don't have a clue about what I'm doing.

► Sometimes I pretend I'm not as smart as I am, especially when I'm dealing with men in business. I'm afraid they won't hire me or want to work with me.

► If I show I'm strong and powerful and really competent and clever, I'm afraid someone will say I'm bitchy, pushy, controlling, demanding. I won't be everyone's favorite, wonderful businesswoman.

What is *your* secret?

THE SESSION

Pretending to Be Less Than You Are

"I just smiled."

"Why?"

"Well, they were discussing strategies for a national conference. I was the only woman in the group, and all the men in the room were sure they were on the right track. I just knew they were missing important elements for the conference to be a success. I made a few suggestions and that was fine. However, in the past with these clients, I discovered they didn't respond well to my criticizing an overall strategy. So I just smiled. I pretended their ideas were fine. I pretended I agreed with them. I often pretend to be agreeable and do things I don't want to do."

"How did you feel after that meeting?"

"Terrible. Frustrated with myself and ready to quit the project. They all seemed so pleased with themselves I couldn't bring myself to push my ideas. I knew it would demand confrontations with some of the men, having to sell my ideas to others. It seemed easier and safer to leave things be. But then after, I don't like how I feel about myself."

"Were you as prepared as you needed to be for the meeting? Did you have some ideas and benefits of those ideas written out prior to the meeting so you could make a brief presentation?"

"No. I've been pretending for so many years that other people's ideas are better than mine, or that I'm not as clever at my work as I know I am, or just that in general I'm not as good as someone else. It seems like that for so many things I do and situations in which I'm involved."

"What do you think would happen if you did show how clever you are, if you did speak up, if you stopped pretending?"

"People won't want to work with me. They won't like me, won't think I'm a terrific team player. Some might think I'm trying to upstage or outsmart them, that I'm showing off. I can still hear that phrase, 'Stop showing off! Who do you think you are?'"

"Do you think they'll start giving female labels to you? Like you're too pushy or picky or bitchy or moody or conceited or it must be that time of the month?"

"Yes, yes, yes. That's a big part of it. And then I don't know how to respond. At the moment it is happening and those comments are made, I feel either too awkward to say anything or I'm just paralyzed. I am really so mad I'm actually concerned I'll really explode and then damage my business relationship."

"You are already hurting yourself. As for the business relationship, you have to have several ready answers so you are not left feeling awkward or paralyzed. You can say, 'I'm sorry you're uncomfortable with my ideas. However, here is why I think this will work better. Let's move forward and see if this fits in the overall plan you have.'

"Unless you are prepared to walk or fight—and you have to know what fights you want to pick—it is best to have several of these types of statements that disarm the situation and put you back in control. At least in control of yourself. You may be nervous the first couple of times you do this, but you'll feel great afterwards. You'll take that strength and courage with you to other situations in your business and personal life."

This was Denise, who started to call me before she went to meetings so she could be reminded she didn't have to pretend to be less than she is. Ever.

We all have heard the type of comments: "When a man is confident, a women is conceited. When a man is worldly, a woman's 'been around.' When a man is a stern taskmaster, a woman is hard to work for. When a man is overreacting, a woman is emotional.

When a businessman is aggressive, a businesswomen is pushy." There's more, but I'm sure you've heard them all. You get the idea.

All too often women fake it in the boardroom and in the bedroom. Remember that wonderful scene in the movie, *When Harry Met Sally*? She demonstrated how a woman could easily fake it with a man in the bedroom. It's also faking it when we just smile and don't say what we really feel or want or need. When we don't stand up for ourselves. When we say, "It doesn't matter."

But it does matter. We are diminishing our power, our resolve, and our opportunities for the successful future that plays itself out in the promises we make to ourselves in the middle of the night. The promises that we are going to make it, that we are going to make our dreams come true!

PRETENDING TO BE MORE THAN YOU ARE

What You Are Is Fine; What You Know and Can Do Is Fine!
Leslie owns a design firm. She's upset and describes how she feels about her work.

> "I convince clients I can do whatever they want me to so they will hire me. I pretend I have plenty of experience and can handle the job when in fact I'm terrified I can't. This is all very new to me. Until a few years ago I had a whole different life. I also kept trying to convince myself that I knew what I was doing. Surely I could easily handle the shift in my life from working for an international company and traveling around the world to being a wife and stepmother living in the suburbs, giving up my job and lifestyle. My office and so-called design studio are in a corner of our two-bedroom apartment. I thought I could do this without blinking!"

I ask Leslie if she's told her husband how hard this is for her. Has she spoken to some of her friends or other family just to vent, to say, "I'm having a hard time," instead of pretending everything is wonderful?

I also tell her how smart and terrific and courageous I think she is. Talk about taking a risk! And even with her pretending and holding in her truths, she moved forward to start a business, joined and became actively involved in a women's networking organization, and started opening up to the women she met who valued her for who she is and what she means to them.

> "I'm beginning to know that you don't have to prove anything to anyone. Having a business has taught me more about myself than anything else in the world I can think of (except marriage). I love it! I've been in Corporate America, and women there are still limited by gender. I truly believe women can fully realize their own potential only as their own boss. I like that all my hard work gets credited to me. I make my own decisions, I can implement my ideas, and my time is flexible to the lifestyle I choose."

We realize that this is why so many women are moving from the corporate world to the world of being business owners. With over eight million women entrepreneurs, and more on the way, there has to be a lot of good reasons. We all know the world of business is compelling—but it has its pitfalls, which I call the three M's: *money, marketing,* and *management.* Still the male-dominated, male-oriented corporate world has yet to open its arms to women at the top levels. And all those barriers and limitations faced on the way up have caused women to say, "Enough!"

"Agreed," says Leslie. "I have no desire to return to that structure, but I have to overcome the stereotypes of what I think a woman business owner should be like."

You also have to deal with the issues so many women in business find facing them: being taken seriously because you're a woman, being asked to do things in business that clients might not ask a man to do (very secretarial activities), and pretending that's all OK. It isn't.

More and more women are determined to create a business environment that is friendlier to women. Women need to set up appropriate boundaries and stop being overly concerned about approval or disapproval. Pretending diminishes your power and your potential.

PRETENDING IT'S OK WHEN IT'S NOT: BEING TRUE TO YOURSELF

Well, I certainly did that for years.

So did Francine.

"Sure, I don't mind that you'll be late for our appointment. It's OK. I don't mind you want to cancel at the last minute; we can just reschedule. It's fine you didn't call me back when you were supposed to. Oh sure, no problem. You asked me to move up the deadline by days. Of course it's all right. I can do that for no extra charge."

"Could I pay you next time we meet? I know I said I would pay you today."

"Sure, sure, sure."

Like Francine, most of us have had these scenarios. We each have our own pictures of how they are played out with various people—from clients and staff to family who don't value what we are doing as businesswomen. We are all too often asked to give too much of ourselves and we keep pretending. No problem. Sure, we can do that!

But we can't!

I told Francine I had been so nice and would quickly say, "Of course, I'll do that" for far too many years. One day, for the sake of sanity and prevention of financial ruin, I said, "Enough already!"

I used to ask a close friend, "Aren't I just as important as the others, whoever the others are? Aren't my needs just as important?" I let others lead when I wanted to. I smiled when I wanted to scream. I acted as if it were fine to be overly imposed upon, treated as if I didn't mind being taken advantage of, with little consideration for my needs and feelings. Sounds like one of our daytime soap operas.

I for one did not and do not want to live a soap opera. When I say no, I don't feel guilty. I don't feel I will be unloved, unwanted, or alone. Women have to take care of themselves without justifying the right to do so. We need to be true to ourselves. In fact, when we are true, we are more secure, happier, more loving, and far less inclined to wish our life were different.

Francine said she couldn't agree more. She vowed she was going to change. She did not want to pretend something was all right when it wasn't. She acknowledged it made her angry.

We spoke quite a few times over a period of several months. She called me after several difficult incidents so she could handle them immediately in a way that made her feel comfortable and good about herself. She began to tell people who were late for meetings her time was also valuable and perhaps they could set a time in the future when they thought they could be on time. She refused to rush her project deadlines without good cause or extra compensation. She's definitely getting the hang of it. She's definitely taking good care of herself and her business.

THE SOLUTIONS

The Orgasm Syndrome! Faking It!

It doesn't belong anywhere in a woman's life.

In business, faking it diminishes who you are and what you want to accomplish.

Pretending you're not as smart and powerful as you really are capable of being, pretending you don't know, pretending to know more than you do, pretending you agree when you don't, pretending you're OK when you're not—all that pretending does little for your business success. Not to mention what it does to your self-esteem.

- ▶ Don't deny your power.
- ▶ Stop pretending you can handle more than you can.
- ▶ Be true to yourself.

Don't Deny Your Power

▶ Ask yourself, "What do I gain by acting less than who I am?" How do you get to have what you want by denying your power in any given business situation?

▶ Make a list of what you've been able to accomplish in your business and personal life and all the things you can do.

▶ Make a list of your skills, talents, and interests.

▶ Get involved in one or two organizations where you can use your skills and talents and be acknowledged for those skills and talents.

▶ Make a list of all that you've learned from your failures and your successes.

▶ Make a wish list of all the successes you would like to have. Think big.

▶ Express your vision of success to yourself, family, friends, and trusted business associates.

Stop Pretending You Can Handle More Than You Can

▶ Next time a client or customer wants or needs something you can't do, tell them the truth: "I can't do it. I won't be able to help you with that." You'll discover not only do you feel better, but also rarely will they run off never to be seen again. Chances are they'll appreciate your honesty and respect you as a reliable and intelligent businessperson.

▶ Find out what really frightens you about being honest. What do you think will happen if you get "caught" and others find out you don't know as much as you think you're supposed to?

▶ Practice being honest with some other businesswomen about several business situations in which you "faked it." Ask them to do the same with you. It might be enlightening for you to see the results of doing this.

Be True to Yourself

▶ Find ways to reward yourself when you have been true to who you are. Buy yourself a present. Take time for yourself. It actually feels good when you don't pretend to be more than you are! Or less!

▶ Express your opinions with confidence. Be prepared for situations where you will be expected to present an opinion or idea.

▶ Stop telling yourself you have to settle for less.

▶ Stop telling yourself you don't have a right to more.

▶ Take walks with friends and talk about how you feel and stop pretending to yourself and to them that everything is just fine. *Everything* is rarely *completely* OK with *anyone*.

▶ Envision your own model of success. Be creative!

MY STORY

I was in my early 30s and decided for quite a few reasons it was time for some therapy. What was a smart woman who was a product of the '50s generation to do with her life?

Betty Friedan wrote about women like me. I felt emotionally and intellectually deprived and, until I became an active part of the women's movement in my mid-30s, I was not sure how to handle my great sense of deprivation. Thank goodness for my involvement in business, which I know gave me some sense of my own identity and self-esteem.

Anyhow back to the therapist. He was wonderful. I will always be grateful to him and the brief time he was in my life.

One day he asked me, "I have to be a guest on a local television show about children and, since you used to own nursery schools, would you join me?"

I was thrilled he valued me in that way. I was excited and nervous. We did the show and I was hooked. I loved doing it. I loved feeling comfortable with it. I wanted to do more. That would eventually happen.

When I met with him a week after the show aired, he said, "You really fooled them, didn't you?"

I said, "I'm not sure what you mean."

"Marcia, you think you fooled people that you're smart. You didn't do that. You really are smart. You know you are. You know what you're talking about. You can't fool people that you're smart. You just are!"

It is one of the best gifts anyone ever gave me. It had become so familiar for me to ignore and deny my intelligence and abilities in order to fit in, and for me to let go of my dreams and ambitions so I would be accepted and perhaps even find great love. When we ignore and deny who we are, there is an innate lie in our relationships and it is difficult to feel much love for others, let alone for ourselves.

I pretended for so long that I wasn't as clever, as smart, as talented, as damned determined to get what I wanted. I pretended it was all right to not act out of being a strong, powerful woman.

When my public relations agency grew to be the second largest in the state of New Mexico within three years, I pretended the business success wasn't all my idea, my work, my efforts. I didn't want to hurt other people's feelings. I didn't want other people to feel diminished by my accomplishments. I didn't want to alienate others because then I would feel alone and alienated. What a terrible price to pay!

What is wrong with acknowledging our accomplishments instead of denying them? We should be proud of what we're capable of and the good things we do. We don't serve ourselves or anyone else in our lives well by being less than we are.

I don't mean we have to act arrogant or unappealingly entitled. I know people who pretend, by acting arrogant or important or as if they could never be wrong about anything. They are difficult, unpleasant, and certainly not especially appealing to be around. That is another type of faking and pretending.

This Orgasm Syndrome is about faking and pretending. It is about us lying to ourselves as well as to others—and ultimately no one wins.

PARTING WORD

STOP FAKING IT! You know all the reasons why.

Session 7
Negative Attitudes

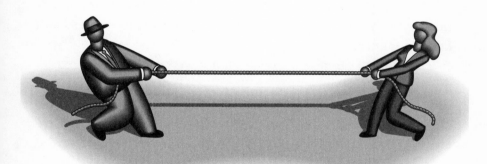

SESSION 7: NEGATIVE ATTITUDES

Success Can't Happen to Me

I'm Not Willing or Comfortable Doing That

It's Not My Fault

Let's talk about what you think could happen if you were a success, if you did things that made you feel uncomfortable, if you acknowledged certain things were your fault

Y ou may have negative attitudes that will defeat you before you even begin. Negative attitudes are a major MindBlock that affects your behavior and your emotions. Ultimately those attitudes interfere with your success and limit your potential.

It's true, of course, that you could have been traumatized by events and incidents in your life. For all of us, they so often become the focus of our thoughts, influencing our actions. We hold on to them like "life trophies"—even when we know they are so detrimental to fulfilling our dreams. How have the women who have made it moved past them or used them as a motivation to succeed? What do you need to do to move beyond your reasons and excuses for having a negative attitude?

UNCOVERING THE SECRETS:
What Reasons Do You Use to Justify Your Negative Attitude?

► I'm angry at my life and lost opportunities.
► I was abused.

- ▶ I really don't want to work or have a business.
- ▶ If I make a lot of money, my husband will think he doesn't have to and I think he should be the one to do that.
- ▶ My husband left me.
- ▶ My husband embezzled from my company.
- ▶ It's my insurance against more disappointments.
- ▶ I have to be the good one in my family; I always have to keep the peace. I can't let anyone see when I'm upset or angry.

What secrets make you feel negative?

THE SESSION

Getting Motivated to Do What Has to Be Done

Remember Wendy Wasserstein's play, *The Heidi Chronicles*? "What do mothers teach their sons they don't teach their daughters?" I have often wondered the opposite regarding women being in business. What do mothers (and fathers) teach their daughters they don't teach their sons?

What I have wondered is why women are taught they can and cannot do certain things. Women have so long been given messages that have affected their attitudes and ultimately their behavior and emotions. How could this not interfere with success in business? How could this not be limiting?

So how do we move past these MindBlocks and eliminate the negative behaviors and attitudes? I strongly believe there comes a time when you have to move past your personal history.

"It has taken me two-thirds of my career to believe in my ability, in spite of obvious repeated successes," Brenda told me. "I think this has been partly my own emotional baggage and partly strong society messages about women as 'helpmates,' rather than initiators and independent drivers. Only when I accepted my own excellence and drive as an integral part of myself as a woman was I personally able to blossom and run my own business with

109

vigor. I work continually to shed self-limiting notions and nourish my creative spirit."

It didn't happen overnight, as Brenda said. We talked about the lack of role models a couple of generations ago, thinking small, thinking someone else knows better than you, that there must be a "right" way to do things. We acknowledged how easy it is to get lost in the world of negativity based on what had been available to women business owners. Even now the system still rewards men more than women: male business owners are taken more seriously, they aren't automatically expected to take care of home and children, and of course, they still have better access to finances.

All this is true and frustrating. Yet our challenge is to eliminate the negative attitudes that can get in our way and stop us from succeeding. The RoadBlocks, which are the external issues, are real; what is even more critical is how we handle them and remove our MindBlocks to success.

We can stay annoyed, angry, and frustrated. We can blame others, complain, and fuss. But what good does that really do anyone? I know venting feels good, and moments of venting are certainly necessary. But by stagnating in that area day in and day out, we only serve to feed the enemy around us and diminish our own presence and power.

GETTING RID OF THE EXCUSES

No More Excuses!

We all have reasons for doing and not doing things, for saying and not saying things. We all can hold onto reasons for not becoming what we want—and at some point they simply play out as a daily melodrama that doesn't serve us well.

It may seem easier to blame others, to complain about women's plight or the competition, to say something is too difficult or takes too much time. The truth is it makes your life ultimately more difficult because you've basically—by your words and behavior—given up. Women manifest different levels of giving up. Some start right at the beginning of a business or project; others reach certain levels of success but are sure they can't be hugely successful or wealthy. Like Dr. Susan Stone.

Dr. Susan Stone is brilliant. She is also continually getting in her own way. She hires people and then doesn't let them do the job she hired them for. She is so sure that no one can do what she wants, that no one can do it as well as she can. She begins with good business relationships and they become bad ones, with everyone angry with everyone. She has been in three-days-a-week couch therapy for years because of her terrible childhood.

It was terrible. I would never diminish that. But she has also used this an excuse for years for controlling everything and everyone she works with. It doesn't take Freud to understand how out of control and frightened she actually feels.

Dr. Stone and I worked together off and on for a number of years. My real appreciation of her work and the fact that I genuinely liked her is some of what kept the relationship possible longer than it should have been. The truth is I was not listening to my own advice because I let my own MindBlocks interfere. I wanted to prove to her I could meet her needs. I could really help her. Well, wouldn't she think I was wonderful?

Finally, even I had enough. It is never emotionally healthy to continually work with someone who makes comments aimed at blaming, diminishing, and discouraging you. Even when you understand the reasons for their behavior, that doesn't mean you have to tolerate it in your life.

We try to make other people change. More often we need to change ourselves. That may even mean changing or eliminating some relationships. We also need to eliminate the negative attitudes and the excuses for not doing what is required to succeed in business. They can take up hours of any day and week and keep you very busy complaining and complaining.

Like Dr. Stone, who certainly had reasons for some negativity in her life based on her childhood experiences, most of us have been impacted by negative voices from our past and our present.

Sometimes in quiet moments alone, Dr. Stone would ask me what I thought she had to do in order to eliminate some of the problems she realized she was causing for herself. We talked about her seeing a different type of therapist. I suggested she trust her judgment when she hired someone and believe the person was competent to do the work that was needed. Then she should allow them the opportunity to prove it. She needed someone to deal with her staff and, with them, set the ground rules, boundaries, work responsibilities, and accountability structure for the business and each individual.

"I can't do it that way. It's not how I want to work. Why should I have to set up my company like everyone else?"

"You don't. You asked me what I thought you could to do make things easier and better for your business. I can't make you do it. You have to accept that things might not change for you and most likely will not if you continue to do things the same way you always have."

That didn't make her very happy. I'm convinced not a lot will.

I love the saying a friend told me: "The definition of insanity is doing the same thing over and over and expecting different results." Susan Stone!

She has so much to offer others, especially other women. What a waste! I hope more women would be less damaged by their past so that they could take positive steps to a positive attitude. Belief in ourselves, fed by praise from those we respect, is indeed the best prescription to cure the negative attitudes.

BELIEVING IN YOURSELF

Can you believe in yourself and accept praise from those you respect?

I've had a business relationship with Sandy for several years. She drives me crazy. She is involved in several of the same women's organizations as I am. She has a constant negative attitude and an "I'm suffering" look on her face. It is so difficult to be around her that many of the other women in the groups do their best to avoid personal contact with her and basically feel she's hopeless.

I know that's terrible. I want all women business owners to feel hopeful. Many of us did try to help her. We met to discuss what she needed and how we could help, offered to help her in various ways for free and to spend time working with her to eliminate some of the problems that interfered with her work.

She cancelled, she didn't show up, she showed up late. We tried again. I know other people outside the group tried as well. Trust me: unless she gets some long-term therapy or someone leaves her a lot of money, she is not going to change.

Sandy told me, "I'm just unlucky." She said she's hoping her luck will change. She's rather like Cher when she said in the movie *Moonstruck*, "I have no luck!" Too many women have waited and hoped for luck to fall in their laps. Success. Prince Charming. An inheritance.

The best phrase I've heard about being lucky is "Luck is being in the right place at the right time." I believe you usually have to make some sacrifices of your time and energy. You have to do the work for it to pay off. You need to believe in yourself in a way that keeps your hope motivated, your energy strong, and your determination positive.

Remind yourself of past successes, stay connected to healthy-minded people, reward yourself for accomplishments, and keep a journal of those accomplishments. These are a few of the things that take luck out of the picture and help you to really believe in yourself and have a positive outlook. SMILE!

Maybe I'll send Sandy a "get well soon" card. Couldn't hurt!

THE SOLUTIONS

It's certainly easy to develop negative or self-limiting attitudes that arise out of our personal histories: a bad marriage, an unhappy childhood, disappointment or even anger about your life circumstances. You may even feel confused or conflicted about what you really want. You may not even have considered success as an option you could have.

There comes a time in everyone's life when they have to move beyond their history, stop holding on to their stories, and choose the life they really want, become the person they want to be. You have to take action to create possibilities ... sometimes massive action.

The solutions to women entrepreneurs' negative or self-limiting attitudes:

▶ Get motivated to do what has to be done.

▶ Get rid of the excuses.

▶ Believe.

Get Motivated to Do What Has to Be Done

Give up Complaining and Being Negative

▶ You have to want your success enough to do what's necessary each and every day. Keep "to do" lists and do what's on them. Check in with positive business associates and with people who value you. If you know Monday is tough for you, plan to do something during the day or that evening that you can look forward to doing.

▶ Don't let a bad moment or disappointment totally stop you. Feel bad for five minutes, then stop that and take some positive actions. Call clients or customers who love your work or your products. Set appointments for new business.

▶ Make a promise to yourself—and keep it—to complain or vent only 10 minutes a day, either to yourself or a friend you can vent to. Then, don't complain or vent again until the next day.

▶ Call a friend or business associate and ask them if you could check in with them daily for positive support. It's difficult to always do by yourself.

▶ Reward yourself for positive actions.

► Acknowledge your personal accomplishments, your personal victories. Thank yourself. Buy yourself a treat.

► Positive thinking and behavior is infinitely better for your business and business relationships. You know how annoying it is for you to be around someone who is constantly complaining, don't you?

► Do a reality check. Remind yourself about all your abilities and accomplishments. Get yourself out places where people compliment you and value your work. We all need positive reinforcement.

► Watch a funny movie. Do not watch a depressing movie about love or life lost. Not if you need your spirits lifted.

► It's helpful if you can remove or limit time with people who constantly upset you, people who make negative comments, who don't support your decision to be in business, who reject or ridicule you.

► Do what you know works to get you motivated. Should you start the day with exercise? What about chocolate? Sounds good to me.

► Get organized.

► Make a plan. What can you do to feel better about what you're doing?

Negative About the Whole Technology Highway?

► Ask your business friends and associates to refer you to reliable and reasonable resources.

► Talk to experts in the field.

► Make a list of what you think you need and what it would be used for.

► Create your list in categories: computer, printer, modem, fax, copier, phone systems.

► Prioritize your list. What is most important? What might be able to wait?

- ▶ If the whole technology highway intimidates you or even scares the heck out of you, ask someone you trust and value to assist you in the planning and buying process.

- ▶ Determine if you will need computer classes. Check out where and who and how much. There are private classes, continuing education courses at local high schools, and "computer geeks" only too eager to show you how easy it is … for them! And I guarantee you, they can help you.

Investing in Technology … an Investment in You

- ▶ Review all the options, costs, payment plans, and what you can afford. Then purchase the best you can manage without causing yourself financial difficulties.

- ▶ Plan courses, classes, private lessons that fit within your budget.

- ▶ Ask someone you know who is computer-literate to help you set up your system and show you how to use your new equipment.

- ▶ Have them set you up with an e-mail address, get you an online service provider and password, and show you how to use the internet for a million and one things.

- ▶ If you want your own Web site, there are various methods and costs. Ask the people from whom you bought your computer or your computer helper.

- ▶ Purchase a book on Internet marketing if you want to promote your business on the Internet.

- ▶ Have a "crisis hot line" to call in case you run into difficulties—your own "computer geek," a business contact, someone in your family, or a friend. Pick up the phone and scream for help before you get too frustrated and want to throw things out the window.

Get Rid of the Excuses

► Sorry! Most people you know are probably tired of hearing about the same problems and stories over and over again.

► Please, understand and accept that most people really don't like being around others who are constantly negative. It's no fun. In fact, it's boring and annoying.

► It will help if you can be honest about what RoadBlocks and MindBlocks are interfering with your success in business.

► It will also help if you're honest about what you get out of being negative. Attention?

► Consider the possibility that negative attitudes or behavior may be the biggest stumbling block of all. Take a good hard look at the excuses you make to yourself.

Believe

► Believe in yourself. You can make it happen. Success is a process. You deserve to be a success.

► Trust yourself to know the best of who you are and that there are just some "yucky" days. You just need to get past and forget them.

► Have people in your life who believe in you, support you, praise you, value you, and treat you with dignity and respect. Have relationships in which you are treated as a priority.

► Teach a course, do public speaking, be a mentor. It is truly energizing and empowering to be in situations where other people value who you are and what you can offer.

MY STORY

Talk about a negative attitude. Me and computers and the whole high-tech highway. I was definitely prepared to stay in my own back yard. I was forced onto this new highway kicking and screaming. Great attitude!

One day when I had a problem with a new printer, I was ready to throw it out the window. My son, the one who lives in New York City, calmly suggested there might be a better option. He is great with computers. That made me even more nuts. Out with the computer, the printer, and the fax machine and time to go back to the Smith-Corona. Those were the good old days.

My attitude about using computers was so negative for so long. I was truly stubborn until I was forced by my own business needs to communicate more effectively and certainly more efficiently. I was going to have to cave in and hit the road.

Doing word processing on a computer was pretty easy. OK, maybe I can do this. Just like typing on any typewriter. But don't ask about the rest, learning how to do inserts, edits, printing, etc. Each step was such a "to do" for me that I sounded like I was building a rocket ship. One day I discovered I could print out an e-mail message. You would have thought I'd just discovered gold.

My son has been patient about all. He once spent an hour on the phone with me when he was in Las Vegas at a meeting. I live outside of New York City so that was an expensive suicide prevention call. I have left messages of my terror at losing a document, misplacing information, needing to put new ink cartridges in the printer, and so on and so forth.

My attitude was so negative I think it's amazing and wonderful how I love using my computer now. I knew I wanted to. I knew I needed to. I knew as a writer I could move paragraphs and sentences from page to page with a few clicks instead of hours of retyping, whiteouts, and carbon paper for copies.

In truth, a negative attitude about anything mostly harms no one more than ourselves. It can be crippling and paralyzing. What really helped me was getting good help and support. From selecting the best computer equipment to being available to answer simple and crisis questions, my son was there for me. We have to know what things are difficult for us and then find the best possible way to make them easier, more possible, and less frightening.

Negative attitudes range from how I felt about technology to how we feel about so much of life and about people issues. Negative attitudes and negative people can take their toll on your psyche and your energy. Don't let that happen to you.

As for me and technology, would you believe I actually have my own Web site? Sometimes I can even find it!

PARTING WORD

No more excuses!

Session 8
8
Bad
Habits

SESSION 8: BAD HABITS

Unprepared, Unorganized, Late, Lying, and Other Outrageous Acts

Let's talk about how you use these to your detriment and to your benefit and how you can kick your bad habits

truly hate when someone is late or unprepared for a meeting with me. Doesn't it drive you crazy when someone you know is always late? What about exaggerating, even lying, to cover up for a mistake or pretending they know something they don't? Couldn't you just shake someone (or wring their neck) who acts totally inappropriately when they are with you at a business meeting or an event?

It may seem a bit dramatic, but the truth is that these things can have a significant impact on you. All too often we women tend to overlook the impact and go on taking care of business. We have every right to expect the people we do business with to be on time, be prepared, tell the truth, and act appropriately. If you're someone who is unprepared, unorganized, late, lying, or otherwise behaving outrageously, you should be aware you are constantly alienating people, damaging your business, and removing yourself from the success path.

UNCOVERING THE SECRETS:
What Keeps Bad Habits in Place?

- ▶ I use it as a good excuse for not doing more or taking on more.
- ▶ I say I'm so busy it's hard to be on time. In fact, I'm really very unorganized, often too depressed to do what's required.
- ▶ I don't have to admit I really don't want to be doing what I'm doing.

- ► I will do anything to avoid conflict and confrontation.
- ► I lie to win a client or an argument. It doesn't matter so long as I win.
- ► Sometimes I lie because doing something like speaking or making a presentation really frightens me. Sometimes I'm afraid of the consequences or expectations of telling the truth.

What are *your* secrets?

THE SESSION

Using Your Time Well and Focusing on What You Need to Do
Pamela is a private investigator who admits she started out with some bad habits.

"I would constantly procrastinate, become distracted by people wasting my time, put off making phone calls to promote my business, and above all, frequently worry about money and get used to making much less than I should have.

"I know my habits were based on my attitude, which was due partly to how I reacted to both my mother and sister, who still do not take my work seriously enough. They judge by how much money you are bringing in. Neither one of them have ever had their own business. They feel I can take off whenever I want to see them because I work for myself. If I worked for someone else, it wouldn't be an issue. And of course there was the juggling of finances and paying out more money than I had coming in because of being a new business."

She decided she wanted to move past these bad habits.

"I began to cut personal expenses and plan ahead until my income was more substantive. Women have to be prepared financially. Starting even a small business can become very expensive. I also realized how important it was to take breaks and be able to get completely away from the business, even a few hours, sometimes a few days. Finally, I asked for help in juggling the everyday tasks. This helped me to stay focused and begin to eliminate my bad habits, which were so distracting and disruptive to my business."

What Pamela began doing was to pay more attention to her own voice and needs and stop listening to others. She said what helped was that her husband was so supportive. By talking things through with him, she began to slowly stop procrastinating and start taking action.

Not all of us have a husband to confide in, but we can talk to a trusted friend or possibly a business advisor to help us redefine our business behavior.

She started networking and brainstorming with others, not just women. "Men as allies are very important too." And she is so right. Good men can be good allies. She found a niche market for her services, established systems to respond quickly to her clients, and most of all listened to others, but decided for herself. "No one else knows what is right for you."

"I also learned through some good advice that I couldn't change my mother or sister but I could change my reaction to them. Having the support of a professional who understood family dynamics was tremendously helpful to me."

For years I have been advising women to find and listen to their own voice. It's that voice talking to you in the middle of the night, the voice chattering away at you all the time. The voice that comes from your heart that tells you to follow your passion. The voice that says you have the right to be what you want and who you want. I know it may take some of us longer than others. The more you listen to your voice and eliminate the MindBlocks from the voices that hold you back, yours and others, the more will power you'll have to eliminate your bad habits.

GETTING ORGANIZED AND STAYING ORGANIZED

"My office is a mess. So is my life. It's just so hard to do all this alone."

I have heard Patricia say the same thing over and over for the past five or six years. Her office is in her home, which means her office, her home, and her life are a mess. I asked a friend who lived near her to help her out for a few days, just to start cleaning up and organizing the mess. He told me I wouldn't believe what a mess it was. I know Patricia is seriously depressed to work and live in such surroundings.

When we first met, we discussed what she needed to do to eliminate the mess, become organized, and stay organized. For Patricia the process of dealing with her real issues was overwhelming. She preferred to drown in the mess rather than face her own truths. She didn't want to deal with the responsibilities and commitments of owning a successful business.

Some women definitely would prefer to be married to a wealthy man than be in business. I cannot change this fact. Patricia is one of them. She wants to be saved! Some days we all do. It's just that for some of us being saved looks different than it does for Patricia. She lives life through the fantasy of an "escape clause" where the dream she thinks will make her happy comes through. Maybe it will. In the meantime she wastes so much of her life falling behind and dealing with the effects of acting frenetic and feeling frustrated in her business.

PROFESSIONALISM AND INTEGRITY

"I must have talked to 300 people today."

"I couldn't call you back."

"I had to rush my dog to the vet."

"The equipment broke."

"I know I should have changed clothes for this meeting, but I was just so busy all day."

Kerri just can't seem to help herself. Everything is a dramatic exaggeration of the day's activities, excuses for not doing what she was supposed to do, stories for delays, and reasons for not being as professional as one would expect for meetings.

She is smart, perhaps too smart. She can outthink a whole lot of people, women and men. Matter of fact, she often outthinks herself into a corner. Even though she does a terrific job as a professional designer, it's difficult to deal with her erratic behavior. It's difficult to deal with and to be around.

I knew she would resent my challenging her excuses and behavior and I felt as if she were going to verbally attack me if I suggested any of this was perhaps not quite true. It's a tough personality to deal with. Who needs it?

Actually Kerri is doing better. She has been in business for eight years and has much more confidence in her ability. That has increased her confidence and self-esteem to the point where she doesn't feel she has to exaggerate so much to protect herself or impress a customer. I see her catching herself, gaining control of what she is saying. She deserves a great deal of credit for having the insights into her behavior and wanting to eliminate what was becoming a serious MindBlock. She began to trust her abilities and her talent and realized she didn't need the exaggerations, stories, and lies to impress anyone. She was impressive enough because of what she created and accomplished.

Not so with Caren. She is so unprofessional in her behavior. She lies about money and payments, lies about credit card debt to her family (who constantly lend her money), lies about the success of her business, lies about her personal life. It took me a while to realize there was little I can do for her.

For me, admitting that is essential to my success and well-being. We all have customers or clients who we know do not serve our business well and we absolutely have to excuse ourselves from doing business with them. I made the mistake in this case of trying for a short while and it came back to haunt me for longer than the work took. Life lessons can be quite amazing. This woman needed far more professional help than could be handled through business therapy.

Sometimes I simply can't help myself. I want to help every woman in business I meet because deep down I know they could become a success. It reflects well on all of us and, as we grow in numbers, we have access to each other in numerous ways that affect the larger picture for all women entrepreneurs: our growing numbers, our impact on the economy of this country, our control over our own futures. Obviously, I'm bound to lose a few, but for the most part I find the majority of women I work with are delighted with the opportunity to have the information, insights, and support.

Many years ago I spent hours working with a woman who owned an educational consulting business. It was a terrific idea and she had all the right credentials. Somehow she just couldn't make a go of it. I fully realized a basic truth a while ago. Being smart is not enough. You also have to *work* smart and *act* smart to be a success. She didn't do either.

Today when I consult with women, I listen and watch for signs of their working smart and acting smart. Hopefully I am able to know the signs and provide solutions to the bad habits that cause them to work and act in ways that are not in their best interest.

Ellen constantly let herself get distracted. She simply loved being in the middle of some activity or another and all too often it had nothing to do with her business. Ellen was a photographer. She was good and was often hired for weddings and big holiday celebrations.

Then there was Mandy, a loud and compulsive talker. She had so much nervous energy and somehow she just couldn't contain her thoughts or remarks. She had a strong opinion about most things and had no difficulty expressing them. Mandy owned a financial business that employed about 10 or 12 people on the average.

I worked at different times with both Ellen and Mandy.

Ellen really wanted to be a success in business. She knew she worked hard and couldn't understand why she had not accomplished more toward her goals. We worked together for several months; throughout that time, I would always ask what she was up to, what projects she had, what she thought she needed. I kept working at keeping her focused. I asked her to be specific about what she was busy with, how many assignments she had, and how she was networking to grow her business.

After a couple months, it seemed to me she was spending a lot of time on projects and "stuff" other than her business. Now, I know we all need escapes and diversions; however, like anything in life, moderation and balance need to go hand in hand with desires and ambitions. Especially if they contradict each other. Wanting to build a business requires a lot of commitment, determination, and time. Being overly distracted by other projects can easily get in the way of business needs.

We discussed how she could be involved in her other interests, with moderation, and dedicate specific hours to them, so her business would not be interrupted by these other activities.

It has taken Ellen more than a year to move away from her many diversions. Much of her involvement was related to being connected to other people, to having them appreciate her and think she was a terrific, concerned, and interesting person. Sometimes she was sure no one else could do what needed to be done but her. We have all learned in our volunteer efforts that's far from true. A little at a time she removed herself from several projects for some organizations, kept a couple that were most important, and most days kept to her business schedule. She made sure her business hours were spaced out in her appointment book strictly for photographic work or marketing her business.

She wanted her success enough to give up her bad habit. That's vital. You have to want your success enough to give up your bad habits.

Then there is Mandy. Just one of those odd stories, as far as I'm concerned. She is a success in spite of herself. She always seems to stop short of doing her best. She also often wears rumpled clothing and acts as if she has no time for anything or anyone. She seems to collect bad habits. Perhaps she actually thrives in spite of her bad habits.

She happens to own a business in a community where she provides good service and the need for that service is great.

She is still loud and truly a compulsive and very fast talker. I once suggested in a polite way that she might soften her tone in conversations and slow down when talking at meetings. I told her she was so smart people wanted to be able to hear clearly what she was saying.

I admire her success. And it's proof that you don't have to be perfect: you can have flaws and still succeed.

Personally I can't spend a lot of time around her. It gives me a headache. I wonder how much more successful she might be if she shed that persona that follows her around? Then again, as I said, she is just one of those odd stories. She continues on her merry way.

So do I!

THE SOLUTIONS

Bad habits in business—like showing up late or unprepared for meetings, using lies as excuses, being disorganized, and behaving badly—are really symptoms that something is terribly wrong. You may actually be under the impression that these behaviors help you to get by, when in truth they are destructive to your business and your business relationships.

Here are the solutions for fixing bad habits:

▶ Use your time well and focus on what needs to be done.

▶ Get organized and stay organized.

▶ Be professional and maintain your integrity.

Use Your Time Well and Focus on What Needs to Be Done

Time Is Money

▶ Be realistic about how much it costs and how much time it takes to do things.

▶ Do you find yourself wasting time and procrastinating? Are all the demands on you distracting you? If you don't already have a good day planner or organizer, get one. Select one whose look, feel, and color please you. Keep a favorite pen in it. Get into the habit of using it to plan and organize your days. *And refer to it daily!*

▶ Allow a realistic amount of time for travel to meetings, clients, buyers, etc. so you won't be late.

▶ If you go from meeting to meeting, don't let them run over and make you late for the next meeting.

▶ Allow extra time between meetings as a cushion and as breathing room for you. Lunch would be good! If you can't finish your business in the time allotted, then schedule another one.

▶ Keep your business meetings moving. When you schedule, ask how long they expect the meeting to take. Or if you're responsible, set the time frame.

▶ If someone is late for a meeting with you and a delayed meeting with that person would throw off your schedule, consider rescheduling your meeting with that person for another time. Or at least call the next appointment, tell them you might be a little late, and ask if that would be OK with them. Most people don't mind and really appreciate the thoughtfulness.

▶ Tell your family and friends what time of the day you are available to talk and what days you might be available to get together. Set some boundaries that work for you and your business life.

Working from Home

▶ If you work from home, set business hours. Don't let family, friends, and personal things you would like to do distract you.

▶ Help plan things for family members that will leave you free to work. I know this is not always fair, but we want to get you what you need. Get childcare, housekeeping, a dog walker, or other help as needed. Ask family and friends to help if you can't afford this, especially when first starting a business.

▶ Set up an office that has a professional look and feel that you enjoy. Set it up so it feels welcoming to customers or clients.

▶ Have separate business and home phone lines. It's absolutely essential for your sanity and well-being. Don't give out your work number to family and friends except in an emergency. Don't give out your home number to business associates.

Get Organized and Stay Organized

▶ Sometimes you have to get important things done you really don't like to do. Prioritize. Do them first and get them out of the way. Think of how relieved you'll be when they're completed. If you have anyone who can help you, ask for help.

▶ Organize your business and your business life in a way that works for you and the whole of your life. I have a business associate who is working toward a paper-free office. I, on the other hand, love my colored writing pads and folders. I have a file for everything. I need to know where I can put my hands on everything.

▶ If you need it and can do so, hire a professional organizer.

▶ In your planner/organizer, keep lists of things you need to do and people you need to call. Keep track of deadlines.

▶ Take off a couple of days or half days to organize your office so it's efficient for you. Make a list of what you need, from new filing cabinets to fax paper. Clean out old files and papers and stock up on supplies. Make up forms that might help you. Be sure your phone and message system works for you.

▶ Be ready for your business. Do what you can afford and keep a list of what you will do as your budget allows. Be creative and resourceful and set up an efficient office or store. If necessary, barter when possible.

▶ If you own a store, step back and evaluate the flow, the appeal, the welcome feeling that should be extended to customers.

▶ Read a book on *feng shui*. I love it! I think it really works. Apparently Donald Trump thinks so too!

Be Professional and Maintain Your Integrity

▶ Be prepared for every meeting you attend.

▶ Do what you say you will do. Keep your word.

▶ Maintain high standards.

▶ Know your facts.

▶ Don't lie. Don't lie about what you know and don't know, don't lie about late deliveries, and don't lie about being late. It makes it even worse.

▶ If you plan ahead and stay organized, you won't have to lie about why you are late or can't make it to an appointment.

▶ By all means, impress people with who you are and what you can do. Just don't take it so far that you end up having to lie about deadlines or projects that don't meet promised expectations. It's sure to disappoint.

▶ Keep your agreements and expect and demand that people you work with keep their agreements with you.

MY STORY

It's easy to think of being unprepared, being unorganized, being late, and lying as bad habits. So are procrastinating and being a perfectionist, just to mention a couple others that come to mind.

When I faced what my bad habits were and how they were interfering in my business life, I had to take a deep breath, ask for help, and be very determined to change my "evil" ways, so to speak.

Overreacting, overpreparing, and overcompensating were at the top of the list. Added to that was my wanting to either impress or shock others. These are not such admirable qualities—and they were all, I realize, behaviors that got me attention and recognition. They also got me a great deal of stress and angst. What in the world was I doing? I needed to give them up, give myself a break, and stop trying to prove something that didn't even matter to anyone else.

I also discovered the bad habit I needed most to put out to pasture was my overthanking, overappreciating, overcomplimenting others. More ways of getting attention or being loved. Good grief! Was there no end to this "woman stuff" I was dealing with?

There was a segment on a television magazine show a number of years ago where a reporter spent a day in an office observing how men and women dealt with each other in the workplace. By the end of the day the women had said, "I'm sorry" or "Thank you" many more times than the men. Rather a telling piece of news. We feel as if we are responsible for anything that goes wrong and need to make all things better.

There was a time my bad habits took their toll on me both physically and emotionally. It's important to be good at juggling many things when you own your own business; however, there comes a time when it can get out of control. My bad habits certainly contributed to my being exhausted and overwhelmed. They also sparked a bit of wishful thinking that if I did all those "over-things," everything would be wonderful. In addition, my overdoing behavior didn't do my self-esteem a great deal of good either.

A bit of insight is always good for what stresses and causes angst. What always seems to help me the most is to vent my concerns and upsets, achieve a clarity about the situation, and then explore good solutions that fit who I am. I knew I could find ways to be competent, prepared, and organized in my business—and even in the rest of my life—without making myself so crazy.

I also simply stopped overthanking and overappreciating. And the more I made myself do it, the easier it became. It certainly became easier to be around me. I stopped going over the edge. I was no longer so crazed from overreacting and overpreparing.

Don't misunderstand. My business style is to be extremely efficient, organized, and prepared. I'm comfortable with that. I'm also comfortable asking for help and setting up systems that provide me with adequate support. And I find in a pinch that a good primal scream while driving down an empty country road or even behind a closed door can be very healing.

PARTING WORD

Bad habits can make for bad business practices and some very bad business decisions.

Session 9
Self-Esteem

SESSION 9: SELF-ESTEEM

I'm Working on Myself
I Feel as if I'm Not Enough
I'm Just Not Happy with What I'm Doing
It Will Never Get Any Better

Let's talk about your identity and image

"**M**irror, mirror on the wall, who is fairest of them all?" We could all take a lesson from the witch in *Snow White* and believe we are the fairest of them all.

So often I hear women saying they don't have the right image, that they're not pretty enough or tall enough or young enough. It hurts my heart and, I must admit, sometimes my own checkbook, that we have bought all of the Madison Avenue advertising hype about how we should look and how we should act. Men don't buy it for themselves and neither should we.

I know: easier said than done. But as long as we look in the mirror and knock ourselves down for not being something different, we diminish who we are and destroy our potential—moment by moment, day in and day out.

UNCOVERING THE SECRETS:
Why Do You Feel Something Is Wrong with You?
Why Are Other People More Deserving than You?

► My background.
► My lack of education.

- ▶ My past mistakes.
- ▶ If I were taller, prettier, and smarter, a rich, handsome man would fall in love with me and take me away from this entire struggle.
- ▶ I feel guilty and ashamed about my character and things I've done.
- ▶ I can hear when people say good things about me. I just don't believe them or feel connected to them.
- ▶ I think I'm really lazy.

What are *your* secrets thoughts about self-esteem?

THE SESSION

"It took me years of being in business to realize what I was doing. If I had it to do it over again, I'd get a better handle earlier. Learning to rely on yourself and your inner voice, to reward yourself and give yourself the praise for the hard things you have to do day to day to be in business. I think the biggest challenges facing women business owners are self-esteem, business and financial knowledge, and family responsibilities."

Alicia has very strong opinions about women business owners.

"It takes courage, determination, the ability to listen and adapt to verbal and physical messages, confidence, optimism, emotional balance, health, energy, resilience. What's more, it takes comfort with chaos and knowing what you want and need."

I often tell women's groups I'm speaking to, "I think women give up their power too easily. Women need to own their power. It's a great ingredient for positive self-esteem." Women need to reach out more to other women in business and to develop closer, more supportive relationships with successful women who value who you are and what you're capable of doing.

"Lack of self-esteem" appears on the top-10 lists for many women entrepreneurs when I ask them about the biggest challenges facing them. While this may not be the biggest issue for the entrepreneur who is grossing in six and seven figures, it is for many who have not reached that degree of financial success and who are in the midst of the "struggling to survive and thrive" attitude in their business.

Volumes of books have been written about self-esteem, and there have been more talk shows and discussions about it than about the coming of the messiah. My particular interest in self-esteem or, more to the point, the lack of it, is its impact on your business.

Clients and customers, employees and vendors need you to be grounded and stable. It's unnerving to constantly be around people who have low opinions of themselves. You can feel their neediness—and it's draining, to say the least.

Over and over, I ask women to think about themselves for a minute. How do you act in business? What image do you present? How do you respond to others? All of these have such a huge impact on how you're perceived and how others relate to you. Self-esteem often grows when we receive compliments for our work and positive responses to our ideas and we allow ourselves to feel good about these things.

We all have our moments of listening to those awful demanding and upsetting negative internal voices. We hear them telling us we're not doing the right thing: "You don't really have enough talent or ability to be in business." You should be with the children more." "You should be cooking pot roast for your husband" (which is great if you want to). "You should be spending more time with your parents or friends." Those negative voices scream at us as we're working and as we wake in the dark of night. They wear away at our self-esteem and damage our souls.

Trust yourself. You have a right to your ambitions and desires. You deserve to feel good about yourself and your accomplishments.

We've all heard the message: self-esteem begins from within. When we present ourselves to others with positive attitude and behavior, at least we stand a chance of receiving positive reinforcement from them.

I also tell any woman who is a boss to compliment good employees whenever possible. Let them know when you think they've done a good job. Let them know you appreciate when they have given extra effort and time. Everyone's self-esteem needs a little boost now and then.

A woman business owner, Marie, from Scotland, wrote and told me how difficult it feels for her.

> "Sometimes what I like least about being an entrepreneur is the loneliness or having to self-motivate. But usually I have a chat with a friend and soon my self-confidence is boosted again."

I can tell you I've been in both places. Self-esteem away on a long vacation and, now, self-esteem in my mind, my heart, and my soul. This is much, much better.

THE SOLUTIONS

All too often, for far too long, women have traded in their dreams of becoming a success at something they loved for the messages given to them by their family and by society. Even today, as hundreds of thousands of women own businesses, they go through life without acknowledging themselves, their powers, their interests, their needs, their true desires.

Many women feel who they are and what they are doing is not enough. There's a daily barrage of messages that if we look a certain way we'll find love and happiness and if we act a certain way we'll be loved and adored. If we act "other ways," we'll be disliked, disconnected, and lonely.

The RoadBlocks of these messages hit us hard as we face our daily business adventures. Our MindBlocks tell us to listen to those messages. Our wisdom tells us better.

The solutions for gaining a healthy self-esteem:

▶ Get another point of view.

▶ Eliminate the internal and external negative voices.

▶ Build confidence and self-esteem.

Get Another Point of View

▶ It's important for your business that you present confidence and self-acceptance. Don't you usually prefer to work with someone who gives you a sense of confidence that they can do what they say they can? Presenting a positive image is essential to success in most businesses.

▶ Do more than work on yourself. Take time for yourself each day. Take care of yourself. Be kind to yourself. Identify with successful people who are similar to you in looks. There are plenty! See, it's not how you look on the outside; it's how you present yourself.

▶ Stop apologizing and being overly grateful. And you certainly don't have to be intimidated by rich, powerful people. You're just as important as anyone else.

▶ This is another good place to make a list of all of your qualities, skills, talents, interests, and abilities. (This is not the time to be modest.) Value all of them.

▶ If you have a truly serious nature, especially when dealing with business issues (like me), you have to lighten up sometimes. Go see a funny movie, watch something dumb on TV, call someone you know who has a good sense of humor.

▶ When someone compliments you, say, "Thank you"—and believe it!

Eliminate the Internal and External Negative Voices

▶ Write down what the internal and external negative voices are telling you. Write all the things you would like to say to those voices. You can save that "conversation" to remind yourself. Or you can ceremoniously throw it all away for good.

▶ Be honest about your character, things that you've done, big mistakes that you've made that you're embarrassed or ashamed of. Be clear about how these negative things came about. Forgive yourself. We all make mistakes. It's having the ability to learn from them and move on that will make the difference between what you have and what you want to have.

▶ Talk about the negative voices. What have they been telling you? How does it make you feel? Don't keep it inside. Be honest about this with people you love and trust. People who love and care about you won't abandon you.

▶ Take responsibility, not blame. If you keep taking blame for things, you may get attention, it may feel familiar, but it's not good for your self-esteem.

▶ Prepare several standard replies for people who make negative comments to you. Sometimes your better customers or clients can be obnoxious and you don't want to lose them. But don't let them get away with it. Having these standard, "protect yourself" reactions can really help diffuse the situation and make you feel better about yourself that you didn't "just take it."

▶ Never, never say anything negative about yourself again—even to yourself.

Build Confidence and Self-Esteem

▶ Be aware of your needs, preferences, and opinions. You have a right to them!

▶ Every day, every week, do several things for yourself and your business—things that you believe in and that you've wanted to do. Prioritize what you want and what you can afford, and then take steps to get them.

▶ Keep track of the positive actions and the positive results, especially in your business. Observe the difference and impact of your new attitude.

▶ Keep a list of your successes. All of them!

▶ Volunteer your time, using your areas of expertise, and see how much people appreciate you. Great for self-esteem. Great for making business connections.

▶ Charge enough for your services or your products. Do some comparison-shopping.

▶ Talk or write a letter to someone you love and trust about the good things, the good results of your business. Share wonderful, successful moments.

MY STORY

When I was younger, I tried to stretch myself so I would grow taller. Then I bought a lot of lemons and tried to get rid of my freckles. I even tried to have my hair straightened once upon a time.

All of this was in vain. I was always going to be "not tall," I was always going to have many freckles, especially in the summer, and I was going to have straight hair only after my hairdresser spent an hour on it.

So once upon a time I wondered, how could a "not tall" Jewish woman with freckles and lots of hair find happiness and success in business? This was indeed a dilemma for me. What to do?

I decided I preferred to acknowledge my good points, appreciate my assets, and be thankful for my positive qualities. If we can't feel good about ourselves and value our strong qualities, how can we be willing to be visible with success, money, and power? How can we have the courage to do what is required to face adversity, cope with challenges, stay on our chosen path, and achieve what we dream and hope for?

It certainly helps and can make a big difference to have people in your life who acknowledge your good qualities and strengths, people who compliment you and support you and help you to know that who you are is enough. Having love and good friends and strong family relationships where you are encouraged, motivated, and appreciated can make a big difference.

Not everyone has that support. It's essential to bring people into your life who value who you are and what you are capable of doing. It's important to have positive voices in your life and make sure you remove the negative ones or keep them at enough distance to not invade your heart and soul.

I once described an upsetting and unpleasant business conversation I had to a business consultant. "I don't get paralyzed into taking action, but this really made me stop in my tracks." What he told me so touched my truths that not only have I never forgotten it but have kept it as a source of coping with ill-behaved people. "What that person said to you," he told me, "paralyzed your heart."

I do have good people in my life who support and believe in me.

I also plan how I can bring my identity to any of my business meetings or speaking engagements. I come well prepared with my business materials and I value my expertise and experience. I like feeling good about my image. That's what works for me, because I know how important it is for me to feel good about myself in those situations. If I don't, I know I may be uncomfortable and not feel as powerful or in control as I like.

Can you just imagine a frizzy redheaded woman, slumped down in a chair, dressed in "yesterday wear," running a meeting or speaking to a couple hundred professional women? I think not.

PARTING WORD

Be the success you want. It's good for your self-esteem.

Session 10

Wishful Thinking

SESSION 10: WISHFUL THINKING

Everything Will Work Out Fine

I'll Think About It Tomorrow: The Scarlett O'Hara Syndrome

Let's talk about why it's difficult for you to look at what's really happening

Remember when Scarlett O'Hara told Rhett Butler in the movie *Gone with the Wind* that tomorrow is another day? I don't know if it worked for Scarlett; it certainly doesn't work for anyone who owns a business. Tomorrow brings a whole new set of needs and possible problems.

Trying to convince yourself that you can put off what needs to be done is beyond simple procrastination. My view of this Scarlett O'Hara Syndrome is that it's "wishful thinking." Thinking that if you ignore it, it will go away, it will be easier another day, or someone will come along and do it for you. Of course, it rarely does go away, get easier, or inspire someone to magically appear to help.

UNCOVERING THE SECRETS:
What Is It You're Really Avoiding/Denying?

- ▶ Confrontation.
- ▶ Verbal abuse or accusations.
- ▶ Facing possible failure.
- ▶ Dismissal by a client, loss of a customer.
- ▶ The time and effort to do it right.
- ▶ Having to acknowledge I was wrong.

▶ Having my version of a nervous breakdown, going over the edge, because of having to deal with all the realities. Sometimes it all feels like too much. I prefer denial!

▶ Lack of trust in myself and my judgments.

What are *your* secrets?

THE SESSION

Faith Needs a Partner—Action

I always thought I could make a lot of money.

I took care of everyone else in my life for a long time before I realized I was about to get into serious trouble.

It was my way of being connected, I thought.

I was hurting myself and the people I loved.

Suddenly the money wasn't coming in quite so fast, quite so easily.

I hadn't saved very much because my own wishful thinking had been "I can always make a lot of money!"

In fact, I was so busy making money and believing, like so many women do, that it was my responsibility to take care of everyone else in my life, I forgot about taking good care of myself. Especially my financial self. This was not an especially fun life lesson. I asked for professional help. I went into short-term couples therapy with the people in my life I love the most and with whom I knew I needed to change the dynamics of our relationship.

For everyone's sake I had to stop avoiding my own truths about money, family, and responsibility. I had to face my voices from the past because I was letting them dictate to me and my life. My financial life and my relationships were suffering. I had to tell those voices rattling around in my mind that I wasn't interested in having them in my life as a powerful force dictating what I should and shouldn't do.

Therapy worked. great!

Truly, our behaviors and judgments are colored by our histories, our desires to please others, and even ourselves. We ignore certain symptoms that mask our truths and we don't pay proper attention to the signs and messages screaming out at us.

Most of the time we know what to do and not do. Often we need support, advice, friends, or family to help us move from our denial.

We can't avoid money matters; business is foremost about money—no matter how much you love what you do. Sometimes we are absolutely unable to avoid confrontation. It's not always a bad thing. It can clear the air and eliminate resentments. We can't avoid what's hurting us, because chances are it won't go away without some effort on our part.

I have always had a lot of faith and hope. I was fortunate to be given that foundation from my family. However, it is only when we put it together with action, and sometimes *massive* action, that we make it much more possible to find success and happiness in our lives.

One of my all-time favorite wishful thinking stories is about two young women who came to me for a consulting session. They wanted to start a daycare center on a very busy main street in Manhattan. It would be a sort of drop-in daycare facility open seven days a week, year-round.

Throughout the conversation there were comments that didn't sit quite right with me and finally, after about an hour, I asked them, "Do you like children?"

"No!"

"How in the world do you expect to have a business like this and make it a success if you don't like children?"

"We plan to hire people to run it."

"Do you have a lot of money to start this center? Do you have family and friends you're planning to have help you?"

"No!"

I honestly was in awe of their wishful thinking. They planned to open this center, hire people, walk away with the profits, and never mind who was running the business. I can tell you I was very concerned about any children being left in their care. Fortunately they never opened this business. I did my best to discourage them, explaining it would probably be several years before they would make enough money so they could afford to hire people to run the center. Chances were they would have to be responsible for managing the business, the money, the marketing, and the children.

Don't misunderstand me. I thought the idea of this type of drop-in center was a decent idea. But coming up with good ideas is rarely the problem; it's facing the reality of what it will take to make them viable.

Faith is great. But remember—it still takes action. Plus commitment, time, and money.

I know in this era of new-age language there's the belief that the universe will provide what you need, some things are meant to be, it's karma. I do not mean to imply this might not be so, only that faith always demands action. This too is a proven rule of the universe. Remember: even prayer is action.

LISTENING TO AND TRUSTING YOUR OWN VOICE

Sally and Margie were business partners. They had started a consulting business to help people tap into their inner selves and discover who they are and how to bring loving relationships into their lives. They are therapists with different approaches, yet similar goals. They long believed they could make a difference in people's lives and created a warm and appealing approach and program.

When we first met, we planned how they could market their concept and what problems they might encounter. How could they achieve their business goals and still maintain their personal styles of being in business? They were excited and hopeful. They were also willing to spend money and time to build their business.

The next meeting they brought a third partner. I knew it was trouble. More important, *they* knew it was. They weren't listening to their own voices and their own hearts. They brought a man into the business; it could just as easily have been a woman who definitely had her own agenda, one that was entirely different from either of theirs, and a mindset that interfered with the entire picture they had presented to me the first time.

It didn't take long to realize the purpose for his participation was financial. He was going to bring additional financing into the project. They were so anxious for the financial help that they just chose to ignore the signs of control he demonstrated. They believed they could control him, convince him to do things their way, and keep him from interfering.

After meeting with the three of them, I phoned Sally and Margie to discuss the situation and hopefully get them to see the inherent danger in bringing him into this project. Not because it was a man. Not because of the money. He simply did not fit into their picture, based on his personality, his behavior, and his action style. I knew it was going to cause them problems. I knew they had been unwilling to think about that or what could happen to their original business concept. The money seemed so important at the time.

"Let's just give him a couple months and see if he stops trying to reinvent the project."

I assured them, "I can give him many months but I don't think it will get better. I'm interested in helping you make this business a success. Your interests are my priority. I know the extra money is important to you right now. Let's explore other financial options. Maybe we could also find ways to reduce some of your costs, delay some expenses, and barter for some services."

I met with them and their new partner several more times. I thought he just kept acting more and more obnoxious and intrusive. He was busy trying to impress me with how smart and clever he was.

Fortunately Sally and Margie are bright women. We agreed to meet a number of times without the new partner and they acknowledged their frustrations and concerns. They admitted they had their heads in the sand because he was willing to invest time and money in their business idea. They were prepared to do whatever was necessary to stop their wishful thinking, stop hoping that it could work out because they wanted it to.

It took a few more months to negotiate with him and make a reasonable and acceptable plan to buy him out and to have Sally and Margie get back to their original plan. It took a lot of their time and energy. But no matter how much they had wished this was going to be a good situation, it was clear to me right from the beginning it didn't stand a chance.

Denial and avoidance: it doesn't work. Somewhere down the road it's going to sneak up behind you and hit you when you're least expecting it to. Neither does it work to ignore your own voice that shouts at you from the depths of your being. Pay closer attention to that voice.

SEND SCARLETT BACK TO RHETT

Once upon a time, women thought their lives depended on the kindness of strangers. They thought they could make it in the world only if they were taken care of by a man who loved them for all eternity.

Honest, I am all for love and romance.

So are a lot of successful women. Only we have learned we can also depend on ourselves. We have discovered we can be taken care of by our own success and financial independence—and have love and romance.

We women cannot live in fairy tales, movie fantasies, or romance novels. We have so much to offer ourselves, our families, our communities. We serve everyone much better when we act out of our own strength and courage, our own abilities and talents. We serve humanity better when we better serve ourselves.

"Frankly, my dear, I don't give a damn," as Rhett said to Scarlett.

As for me, I don't give a damn that I have occasionally been accused of being addicted to helping women succeed. This is because I do give such a damn about women having business success that brings them economic security and financial independence. I give a damn that businesswomen are taken seriously.

Donna did not have a lot of money and she had even less cash flow. Not an unfamiliar theme for many entrepreneurs. Often women entrepreneurs have the added burden of being a single mother, less access to investment dollars, and difficulty being taken seriously.

Still Donna spent many hours working on her business, seeking my advice, and having a rather good sense of hopefulness. She determined she wanted a Web site, which in this new age of technological advancements seems almost commonplace. The only way she would be able to have one developed for her business, she determined, was by bartering with someone. She was a healthcare consultant and figured if she could find someone who could be interested in what she offered and benefit from it, the barter could be a good move.

Well, it should have been. It could have been. Except for one minor detail. It took them months to accomplish what should have taken only a few weeks at most, and she was frustrated and angered at having to constantly cajole, appeal, and sometimes demand what she had been promised.

Often when entrepreneurs barter, it's really with a great sense of wishful thinking.

As with Donna.

> "I know he is really a good person and wants to do a good job for me, so he is taking his time. I think if I just let him know I value him and that I understand how capable he is, he'll just come through for me. I don't want to be too pushy because then he might not want to do it at all."

It's easy at first to ignore the signs of not being treated in the way you should expect—professionally, work done on time, your phone calls returned in a timely manner. After a while you become annoyed, then a little while later frustrated, and soon enough plain old angry. I've been involved with enough barter arrangements in hopes of getting some work done I need while holding on to my cash. It works only when both parties act in an honorable way. The problem with most of us is we know within a short time if we like working with someone, if we really trust them, and yet once we might realize we don't, we keep giving them enough rope to hang themselves—and us as well.

> "I know he is totally crazed with all he has to do. I know he means well and I just hate to push him," Donna related to me at one of our meetings. "I think if I give him some time he'll do this the way I want. He promised me I wouldn't be disappointed. Of course I'm annoyed and frustrated. I just want to give him a chance."
>
> "Have you told him you are now on a tight deadline?"
>
> "Of course."
>
> "Have you asked him to give you a drop-dead date that he will have this completed?"
>
> "Of course."
>
> "Do you think he will meet that date?"
>
> "Well, I think he wants to. And I'm not sure what I would do if he doesn't."
>
> "Actually, I don't think he will. I don't think he really cares. I think he got what he needed from you. I think he rarely honors his agreements, I think he messes up for his customers a lot, and I think the only way you will get him to complete this work for you is by telling him that if it isn't done by a certain date you are going to the Better Business Bureau, the local Chamber of Commerce, and the local newspapers to give them all the story of how he does business."

Even when you're involved in a barter business arrangement, you have every right to expect to be treated fairly and equally as any other customer or client.

Donna, with a lot of encouragement, finally pushed and warned him, as I suggested, that this was totally unacceptable and she would go to the Chamber, etc. I know it was difficult for her; by nature she's trusting and generous. She also wants to believe everyone is good at heart. I've been in business too many years to believe that fairy tale.

THE SOLUTIONS

We know it can be difficult to start and grow a business. There are RoadBlocks everywhere a woman turns. Personal demands, competitive disadvantages, fear of consequences if we take certain actions, and lack of money can be exhausting and frustrating. It's easy to understand why one could find some appeal in wishful thinking.

Here are a few examples of wishful thinking: believing just because you work hard you'll get a lucky break, ignoring signs of serious problems in the hope that they'll just go away, wishing Prince Charming would rescue you, and simply telling yourself you don't want to think about it today. Wishful thinking is believing that the universe will magically provide for you.

Faith definitely needs a partner—action! As you've seen throughout this book, you can overcome the MindBlocks and RoadBlocks to success. Stop the wishful thinking; it doesn't belong in business.

The solutions for taking charge and not indulging in wishful thinking:

- ▶ Face the problems.
- ▶ Have some street smarts.
- ▶ Do what's necessary.

Face the Problems

- ▶ Look at what's really going on. Get a good handle on your business.
- ▶ Where do you feel vulnerable as a businesswoman? What are all the things that could go wrong? Are you relying on dependable people? Are you relying on money to come in that

might not? Are you ignoring your instincts? Are you avoiding calling someone and handling a difficult situation?

▶ Acknowledge any ways in which you indulge in wishful thinking.

▶ Face actual or potential problems and reach out to professional resources who can assist you with them. It could be an accountant, an attorney, or a business consultant. Ask business associates for referrals. Utilize women with whom you network. Ask for references, fees, and credentials. Work only with people you are comfortable with and have confidence in after interviewing them.

Have Some Street Smarts

▶ Trust your instincts.

▶ Stay informed of your business environment and trends. Read your trade publications and local and national news. Listen to your clients, customers, and associates. What is happening that you should know about that can impact your business? What changes are occurring in your industry that can adversely affect your business?

▶ Are you denying what's happening? Do you have your head in the sand? Take it out! Make plans to expand, diversify, reduce inventory, even consider a partner or some other strategic alliances to bring in more business.

▶ Spend adequate time preparing and following up on important proposals, presentations, promotions, and other business initiatives.

▶ Take good care of existing business. Clients love check-in phone calls, thank-you's and prompt replies to their calls. Customers love things like complimentary coffee, frequent purchase cards, and understanding replies to their returns. Unless they return frequently!

▶ Are you doing everything you possibly can to be sure people know about your business? Are you doing enough public relations and advertising? Do you have adequate sales and promotional materials? Do you need someone to help you get press releases into local papers?

Do What's Necessary

▶ Be alert to problems and challenges.

▶ Be prepared for consequences. Handle them before they become a crisis.

▶ Protect your interests. Have a backup plan.

▶ Know you have to save yourself. Don't wait for someone else to save you.

▶ Don't procrastinate. It can only get worse.

▶ Learn to work *smart* instead of *hard*!

MY STORY

When I started my first marketing/public relations business, I was working for a television station as promotion manager. I told my boss, the station general manager, that I was going to start a public relations agency and I wanted the station to be my first client. I would do almost everything I was doing as a full-time employee for half of the salary he was paying me. He thought about it for a few days and said, "Yes." What a great way to secure other clients—telling them the number-one station in the market was my client. Actually, I thought it was a pretty smart move, if I must say so myself.

If I was so smart, then how come I would find myself in situations where I gave away my power? I have long discovered *being* smart is not the same as *acting* smart or *working* smart.

I would say, "I can't handle all this, there's too much to do," and I would accept advice or help or information from the wrong people. Of course, there was also wanting to be connected to people if I was feeling especially vulnerable or even lonely and sometimes I made not so smart choices. Then I would be in situations where I allowed my wishful thinking to believe that they would make everything all right. Yet, at heart, I knew if I listened to my instincts, to what my own voice was telling me, I would have made better business decisions. I would have taken better care of the finances, the clients, the projects.

"How true," most people comment when I tell them this story.

When we don't pay attention to our instincts and we avoid responsibility, we can end up in some serious business trouble. I've put myself in harm's way several times because I didn't want to hurt someone else's feelings or I ignored the truths I knew about their abilities or areas of expertise. My wishful thinking was leading the way. I wanted to believe things would work out. I wanted to believe everything would be fine tomorrow and tomorrow. Me and Scarlett.

By the way, I once started a make-up company called Scarlet Natural Cosmetics. The slogan was "Be a Scarlet Woman"—but that's another story.

PARTING WORD

Pay attention and be responsible to your business. Ignoring problems only causes much bigger ones.

Session 11

Preventing and Handling Crises

SESSION 11: PREVENTING AND HANDLING CRISES

Financial, Emotional, Physical

Let's talk about your business life

Why do women find themselves in the business predicaments they do sometimes? Certainly we are smart enough, we are not lazy, and in fact we seem to be rather bright and ambitious. Yet we have these MindBlocks and RoadBlocks that cause us great harm at times, especially when we don't pay attention to a disaster in the making and the unpleasant and unacceptable results when a crisis is upon us. It is necessary to pay attention and be accountable for details, finances, people who work with us and for us, the marketplace nuances and shifts, what is required for what we want to accomplish. A crisis can appear in "many-colored coats" and leave us stunned at the impact on our business and our lives.

You can't ignore when your cash flow is poor, your account is overdrawn, you've missed a deadline, a client or customer is upset, you have little new business on the horizon, and other such business headaches. If you ignore them, you're bound to have a crisis of major proportions giving you an even bigger headache.

UNCOVERING THE SECRETS:
What Stops You from Taking Measures to Prevent Crises?

- ▶ Sometimes I'm so confused and I don't feel I have anyone I can talk to about what's happening, about what I need, without feeling embarrassed or uncomfortable talking about my situation.
- ▶ I feel as if I don't have the right to burden others with my difficulties or concerns.

► I think if I talked to people whose opinion I value, they wouldn't want to be bothered with me or I would feel as if I'm annoying them.

► A lot of the time I just don't know what to do and where to get help and I'm not even sure what I need. I feel pretty stupid saying I need help when I don't know what I need it for.

► I find it difficult to justify doing certain things, especially when it comes to taking time to take care of myself and my business. I also know how ridiculous this sounds.

What are *your* secrets about dealing with crises?

THE SESSION

The right support systems, attitudes, and valuation of one's past successes are important guideposts for dealing with crises, as well as for preventing and surviving them. Because women are usually so concerned with how other people respond to them, they tend to fall into the trap of forgetting or putting aside their own business needs.

Some people love to live on the edge. The only problem is you can fall off. Sometimes the fall brings only mild injuries, but other times it can be life threatening. When a crisis occurs where there is a risk of losing your business or all your money, I have no doubt it feels like a life-threatening situation. Like any life crisis, it takes all your energy, will, and resources to deal with it effectively.

Victoria had been a successful designer for more than 25 years. Her designs were in Fifth Avenue stores and high-end boutiques and she commanded a top price.

"Somewhere along the way I was so involved with the details I stopped looking at the big picture. I was always more interested in the designs than accounting systems or financial statements. I certainly knew I was making a lot of money. Still, I was more interested in the final product than the costs of the materials or price comparisons with similar product lines. And because I never had a financial problem with my business, I just assumed all was fine. By the time I realized I was in trouble, I was in *big* trouble. It was a combination of many factors that came together at one time. Ultimately I was facing bankruptcy, possibly closing down my company, and every day dealing with the crisis. It was draining and took all my strength and energy to keep working while dealing with the problem at hand."

Victoria and I were friends. When she finally spoke to me about what was happening, it was with great difficulty. I knew she felt embarrassed. She was also angry: angry with herself for not paying closer attention and angry with the people in her company she felt should have been protecting her and her business. Once the conversation moved past the upset, we reviewed what she was doing and planning to do to deal about this situation.

I suggested some professional contacts I thought might be able to help her financially and we came up with a list of other people who might be able to provide her with additional resources. She was in the process of revising her business plan, organizing her business so it could possibly be sold with her remaining as the head designer, and seeking financing through various avenues.

Most important, she never quit. She was often frustrated and even at her wits' end at times. She went from anger to tears, from upset to being adamant about finding a way to save her business.

"I knew if I quit I would feel terrible. I was determined to do everything I possibly could to save my company and my reputation. Lucky for me I have a real soul-mate husband who also never gave up on me and constantly supported me, especially emotionally. It was a tremendous help to have that kind of support and I think other business-women who go through this type of experience without it must find it almost impossible to deal with the problems."

Well, not impossible, but without a doubt significantly more difficult. We all need those right support systems; they give us strength and hope and encouragement. Sometimes it can be a friend or other family member; sometimes it can be a business associate or even a consultant who has a particular expertise to work with you in solving the crisis. But it's the day-to-day dealing with the crisis that shows our merit.

Every one of us can quit at any given moment. That's the easy thing to do. Victoria had no intention of doing the easy thing. She kept her determination: she ultimately arranged for financing and sold off part of her company. Maybe it wasn't ideal and surely she would have preferred it never happened. Yet her greatest triumph is that she not only succeeded in not falling off the edge but also managed to climb back up on top, where she deserved to be. She's a wonderful person and an extremely talented designer.

Then there is Jenny, who is always ready to jump off the edge and blame everyone else for pushing her. I am absolutely convinced her middle name is Crisis. Everything becomes a crisis with her. Jenny's attitude is "They made it happen," and she refuses to look at the truth of how "it" actually occurred. She drives everyone around her crazy and more often than not so alienates the other businesswomen who come into her life that she is left alone with her numerous crises.

Last time I spoke with her, I asked her what she got out of behaving the way she does.

> "You must get something out of this. Attention? Jenny, you have to make choices in life and that holds true for your business life as well. You have to understand the impact of your choices because you have to live with them and, as is so often the case with you, to deal with a crisis you've caused."

I've been having business crisis intervention conversations with Jenny for two years and I decided I needed to be very honest with her. Maybe someday she would get help with her emotional issues, those interfering MindBlocks, and not need a crisis to get attention or give her life some meaning or purpose.

She was not very happy about this. There are people who love being in a crisis. Their neediness is maddening. The phone calls, the conversations, the suggestions—so much time and energy spent on them.

Jenny owns a small service business connected to a larger national company. She has problems with the people she works with and for, she has issues with the paperwork and being organized, and she is always late, always just making a deadline and always acting as if she is the only one who has so much work to do.

I've told her on a number of occasions most women entrepreneurs are burdened with too much. We work long hours, sometimes get treated unfairly, come home to more work, and sometimes even get treated unfairly again. We all have to figure out how to find a balance in our lives and ask and expect people we live with and work with to respect us and take us seriously. People in constant crises often don't even want help. They prefer the crises to happiness and success.

I also know this isn't true for everyone. Some women seem to have more than their share of bad situations and I am always amazed how they refuse to give up, quit, or fall off that edge. They have a hidden strength and determination. They have good coping skills and people resources.

Cindy lost her business, her homes, and in the process her lifestyle.

> "I didn't pay attention to my gut feeling about what was happening in my business. Whenever you don't listen to that feeling and go to the intellectual, I think all is lost. It was for me. I trusted people I shouldn't have. I made excuses for them. I didn't stop the crisis from coming, because I didn't want these people to think I didn't trust them or have confidence in them. I paid a big price for this thinking. I will never let it happen again. I know I have to be responsible and accountable and so does anyone who might work for me."

She has been struggling ever since to "survive and thrive." She's done what she's had to in order to earn a living. She's started a small service business out of her home. She's joined business organizations and women's networking groups, where we met. I offered to help her because I knew she was willing to help herself. Even though she was devastated by her losses, she didn't constantly complain. She never gave up on reestablishing herself as a successful businesswoman.

I provided her with some marketing ideas. She spent money on brochures and business cards. She took classes to expand her knowledge in a field of work that truly interests her. A little at a time, she's rebuilding her life and her quality of life. She deserves a lot of credit for her mindset. The RoadBlocks were significant and yet she continues to keep a positive attitude.

Sometimes a crisis is caused by an addictive behavior that is so pervasive it takes over one's very being. It could be gambling, alcohol, drugs, even food. This is certainly not an issue for a business therapist; it is for professionals who deal with emotional and psychological issues and for those people who work for programs designed to help people face their personal demons and challenges. The impact on their business can be staggering, with enormous losses. Help is always just a phone call away.

I know it's not as simple as that to take the right actions. Any woman who finds herself in need of this type of help and support should know we appreciate how courageous she is to pick up the phone and say, "I need help!" In one way or another, we all do.

Difficult people can certainly cause us to have a crisis. They are upsetting and infuriating and I think they love to be provocative and cause melodramas for themselves and others.

Poor Rhonda! When she started telling me about her problems with Susan, I felt like I wanted to help Rhonda wring her neck. Susan was upsetting, infuriating, provocative, and more. She had such little concern for others, being so self-absorbed in her own daily melodramas, it was nearly impossible to deal with her on a rational level.

Rhonda was involved with her in a project and needed Susan's access to a group of people whom Rhonda was hoping to bring together for a major event.

"We agreed to meet late one afternoon to talk about how this could work and what she needed me to do. I said she should tell me what was best for her, I could be flexible. I arrived a few minutes early, compulsive as I am about all this. She arrived nearly a half hour late. By then I was uncomfortable sitting alone in this bar/restaurant, getting angrier by the minute, and suddenly she comes sauntering in with little apology, only how she is always so busy and it makes her late because of it."

Rhonda continued telling me about this meeting.

"At some point during the meeting, I asked her for the list of names she had so I could add them to an invitation list and she felt she just couldn't do that. I asked her if I could attend one of her planning meetings and again she slowly, ever so slowly, told me, "Probably not a good idea.' 'Well, what can you do?' I asked 'How can you help with this other project? If you want me to do some things for you, I need you to be willing to help me a little with this other project.' She proceeded to get annoyed and then nasty. I don't know what her problem is."

I happen to know Susan. I know she is seriously depressed and hopeless. She holds on to an anger that just won't go away and in the process she seems to get great pleasure in being provocative, stirring up trouble wherever and whenever she can. It's lots of little comments, interruptions, disruptions, and rude comments under her breath. She loves to attempt to cause a crisis by asking questions and making comments that could stir negative emotions and initiate a conversation sure to create controversy. She drives all of us crazy with her nonsense!

However, that doesn't mean we don't have to deal with it, because we do. It doesn't mean we can just let her go on and on and cause a crisis. I find I am constantly aware of having to prevent a crisis when I am in her company. Rhonda and I talked about this after one of her attempts at troublemaking times.

"You know she is just so angry," Rhonda said, "that she wants to make everyone else miserable by acting out of how right she is about something or other.

"Knowing it doesn't make it any easier. She makes so many situations tense and stressful when it is so unnecessary. Then someone is left trying to divert a disaster. So many women I know just don't want anything to do with her because she seems so bitter and constantly complaining about something. It's just the worse part of it is the problems it could cause at any given time."

"We all know that, Rhonda. Susan is in need of serious help. She and I have spoken on several occasions and I don't know that any of us can really do the job. Some people are just determined to stay stuck in their messes and at some point we need to know to leave them be and hope for the best for them."

On the other hand, I would still like to wring her neck!

THE SOLUTIONS

Any business crisis can stop us in our tracks. Crises can happen all of a sudden. Often they are a result of not planning or preparing for business needs and problems. From cash flow and other financial issues to delivery delays, from changes in the market to changes in your own marketplace, crises arise and you need to cope with them. Preventing them when you can is the best of all possibilities. Preparing for them is simply smart business.

By *not* eliminating the MindBlocks and RoadBlocks associated with owning a business, a woman entrepreneur can herself create one type of crisis or another. Money, feeling exhausted and over-whelmed, relationships, sexism, fear and anxiety, being a pretender, negative attitudes, bad habits, lack of self-esteem, and wishful thinking—they all present real challenges to your business success.

The solutions for surviving and thriving in business:

- ▶ Prevent crises.
- ▶ Prepare for crises.
- ▶ Cope with crises.

Prevent Crises

- ▶ Address the common MindBlocks and RoadBlocks in this book. Work through each issue that concerns you. Follow the proven, practical solutions.
- ▶ Know that most crises can be prevented by paying attention to your business, your industry, and your instincts.
- ▶ Keep an eye on your competition—what they offer and what they charge.

Financial Controls

- ▶ Establish a financial controls system in which you are always aware of your financial situation.
- ▶ Be aware of cash flow, expenses, and income.
- ▶ Review annually or semiannually whether you're charging enough.
- ▶ Send invoices out on time. Make collecting money a top priority. (Refer to *Session 1: Money* for more information about getting paid and other financial solutions.)

Prepare for Crises

- ▶ Have a source for a short-term loan during cash flow difficulties. Check with your bank, your business advisor, your family, or some business associate you may have a good relationship with. If you have decent credit, you might be able to get a line of credit from a bank or an extension on a credit card.

▶ Use credit with great care and caution!

▶ Use independent contractors as backup for employees and to handle overflow work—especially helpful when employees quit or suddenly become ill. Many women who own service businesses can fill a temporary void for your business or perform necessary services reasonably and quickly.

▶ Build a file of résumés in case you need help quickly.

▶ Build a network of people who can help, provide referrals, and lend support.

▶ Implement a system for checking and developing all areas of your operation, from business concept to communications, accounting to personnel, marketing to fulfillment and delivery, etc.

▶ Meet with employees regularly. Discuss any problems or issues you should be aware of.

▶ When you suspect a problem, take immediate action. Don't put it off thinking it will just go away or that maybe it's not really a problem. It may not be a serious problem, but find out for sure.

Avoid Personal Crises

▶ Take good care of yourself. You're the boss.

▶ Stay focused on what you're doing.

▶ Protect yourself from being overwhelmed by other demands.

▶ Leave time for what you need to do for yourself and for your business to succeed.

▶ Avoid working late too often.

▶ Take breaks during the day, throughout the workweek.

▶ Take vacations. If you can't afford to, take short day trips.

▶ Stay in touch with friends. Stay connected to good people.

▶ Ask for and expect good help at your place of business and also *at home.*

Cope with Crises

Get Help

▶ Recognize that you don't have to go through a crisis alone or have all the answers all ready! Again, this may be a time to call your lawyer, banker, or other business advisor.

▶ Ask vendors and other business associates for information and help.

▶ Get free counseling and advice from nonprofit organizations. There are women's organizations now for almost every industry. Most have excellent resources, programs, and information. They are there for you. Put any embarrassment aside and ask to meet with an expert in an area you need advice with. Nationally, the American Women's Economic Development Corporation in New York City does one-on-one counseling, both in person and by phone, even long-distance. They offer excellent seminars and training to help you to succeed in business. It's worth a phone call.

▶ Get information from books, magazine articles, and the Internet. If you have a computer, you can go online and specifically research women's books, resources, and organizations.

▶ Develop good coping skills.

▶ If you're the type to react with melodramatic behavior every time there's even a minor crisis happening or on the horizon, give it up. You're driving people around you nuts! It's not worth the attention you're getting, because most people wish they could be far away from you and this behavior.

▶ Have suitable outlets for your embarrassment, fears, angers, and frustrations. Scream and cry in private. Try meditation, yoga, or Reiki. Work it out with some physical activity.

MY STORY

I don't like having a crisis.

I used to!

I think the best thing about me and crisis is my parents somehow gave me the ability to cope, think on my feet, and move into action when necessary.

I believe in being prepared.

I keep the car full of gas when we're expecting storms and in case I need to escape somewhere away from this oceanside community.

I like feeling centered.

I appreciate having good people in my life who can help me when one of life's little emergencies appears. They are different from a real crisis and having help in these situations prevents the little emergencies from becoming crises.

I believe in preventive measures, from health to business. I am very fortunate. I have one son I can discuss health issues with and the other son business issues and even more with my terrific women friends.

Sometimes I push too much. Many of us do. I remind myself to stop, slow down, and take care of me. Falling apart in any way is quite an obstacle to success. I know I can't control natural disasters or the natural progression of life. But I know I can prevent *unnatural* disasters if I pay attention and act responsibly.

PARTING WORD

Run away if you want. But come back soon!

Session 12
Success

SESSION 12: SUCCESS

I Really Want It

I Really Deserve It

Let's talk about how to be comfortable with success, your business savvy, some of the unwritten rules

The triumph of American women entrepreneurs is enormous. Because of their daring, the progress has been tremendous. They have changed the social, financial, and political position of women for good, and they can now feel assured that their ambitions and dreams can take them anywhere they want to go. What an enormous impact women entrepreneurs have had on women's lives! What a huge impact on the economy!

Yet women entrepreneurs, the daring risks they have taken to achieve their success, and what it means for women's lives have not been fully acknowledged and celebrated. Realizing the significant and positive changes their efforts have had is a strong motivation to get beyond the remaining MindBlocks and RoadBlocks to have more success and happiness in business.

UNCOVERING THE SECRETS:
What Really Stops You from Doing What's Necessary to Be a Success?

- ▶ I might really succeed and then have to be responsible and accountable for that success.
- ▶ I'm not sure I feel I deserve to be a success.
- ▶ My relationships with my family and friends will change.
- ▶ I wouldn't have time to garden, shop, go out with my friends. Maybe I just want to be a wife and a mother.

What are *your* secrets?

THE SESSION

"I own a contracting business, which is rather unusual for a woman. Although frustrating at times, I persevered, always having to do a better job than anyone else, until more and more opportunities arose. I won't quit. I believe it takes focus, dedication, and belief in one's ability to be successful. I define success as being a player for more than 10 years."

—Joan Stern

"I started out teaching English Composition and Women's Studies, but found it boring and unrewarding. I was offered a job as advertising director of a weekly newspaper, having no idea how to do the job. I learned on my own and, after six years, an artist and I founded our own advertising agency. The business has grown steadily for the past 11 years. Four years ago I bought out my partner when she moved out of state. We have won awards, kept our clients and accounts for a long time, and are by industry standards successful. To be successful I think it takes confidence, talent, intelligence, and above all, the ability to laugh at oneself. I define success as creativity that's good enough to command respect and a substantial fee."

—Teri Bardash

"There is no single 'thing' that contributes to a woman's success as an entrepreneur. However, some of the contributing factors include having a product or service that people want to buy, a really strong network of people who believe in your product or service and refer business to you, and most important, I think, a personality that is sincere, outgoing, and friendly, so people trust you. To me personally, success means ... ease of doing business and feels like it's worth the wait."

—Lucy Rosen

"I wanted to help people—with a passion. I was lucky nothing could stop me! I wanted to be the best psychotherapist. All the conflicts, familial and social, could not stop me! I cried and cried, then got up and went on. There is nothing worth having that does not involve hard work. For me success meant passion, ambition, vision, and money. I define success as comfort with self, knowledge of self, and clarity of purpose. Money usually follows."

—Joan Fallon

"A message to any women becoming an entrepreneur. Look at both sides of your life, the business and personal—what it is you want to achieve for yourself, what things success will bring you, what things you will not have, like time for other things—and ask yourself whether you can be happy with that. To be a successful entrepreneur, you have to be willing to make sacrifices that may mean less family or personal time. Accept that and be happy with what you do and the time you do have. For me success is being a well-balanced person, happy with success in both business and personal life."

—Lisa Vaccaro

"Success for me is reaching my goals and keeping my sense of humor. It takes a willingness to work long hours, a can-do, happy attitude."

—Marilyn Butz

"Drive, talent, persistence, people skills, dedication, ability to be detail-oriented and systematic, and marketing sense are essential traits for business success. I also think it's important to network with other like-minded women. You have to connect with others, since self-employment can be very isolating. Take time for yourself; it actually can make you more productive when you feel good about yourself. Success? Well, gratification, happiness—and a nice paycheck doesn't hurt either."

—Robin Gorman Newman

"Traits of success: Determination. Confidence. Stubbornness. Farsightedness. A desire to succeed. A willingness to learn more. A humility to learn from mistakes made. As for my idea of success, it's being happy and content with life. Being self-sufficient financially—not burdened with debt. Providing a loving and secure environment for your family and enriching the lives of others. I think that if you believe in yourself and have confidence in your business you will succeed."

—Marie Breward

"I want to be the next Lillian Vernon. To have that type of success takes persistence, optimism, flexibility, and a hunger maybe. Also, I have a dread of returning to the corporate rat race."

—Liz Matt

"Freedom. Freedom to be able to do what I want."

—Pamela Shenk

I've asked many, many women over the course of writing this book, "What is your vision of success?" The answers I've received varied little from woman to woman, business to business. Financial security, independence, and being taken seriously are recurring themes.

I've also asked, "What qualities do you think a woman needs for business success?" The answers: money, determination, courage, confidence, support, intuition, the ability to cope with adversity, and a willingness to develop supportive relationships.

Other women have told me, "Success isn't just about money; it's also about knowing what level of business success makes you happy. It's about balancing personal, family, and business life."

My view of success is that it is the positive outcome of incredible, exhaustive, and determined efforts. For me the rewards are a great bounty of economic security and freedom, credibility, joy at doing what I love to do, and a strong sense of well-being. Success is a prize that drives most of us entrepreneurial women. Apparently millions of women who own their own businesses feel reaching for the prize is worth the effort.

THE SOLUTIONS

Over the past two decades women entrepreneurs have changed the landscape of the business world. We have created our own models of success and established ourselves as a group of entrepreneurs who expect and deserve to be taken seriously.

Traditional expectations and roles since the beginning of time, it seems, which had been a major RoadBlock for women's business success, have taken a back seat to our value as breadwinners and our leadership qualities. Through hard work, determination, networking, communication, and creative problem solving, as well as strength in numbers and many excellent women's business organizations, women have found ways to set up their businesses and their lives in ways that make business success possible.

Women entrepreneurs have laid a solid foundation of success these last 20 years. In many ways, it is true that women entrepreneurs can have it all. But not one woman I know—including me—has ever said it's easy!

Solutions for success:

▶ Establish a success that fits who you are.

▶ Invest in your success.

▶ Sell yourself and get connected.

Establish a Success That Fits Who You Are

Eliminate the MindBlocks and RoadBlocks

► Know what stops you or causes you the greatest difficulties. Be honest about the mindsets and secrets you have that interfere with you doing what's necessary to achieve the success you want and deserve.

► Find a way to get to the heart of the matter for problems that come up. Talk to someone. Write about your thoughts and feelings. Know what makes you upset, frustrated, and stressed!

► Let this book help you.

► Know that there are times when you will need to give up being "right" in order to win.

► When one of your symptoms appears, ask yourself, "What is this really about?"

Have a Success Plan

► Write a plan that details your idea of success. It's helpful to know what you really want.

► Define your business goals. How much money do you want to make? What do you want to accomplish?

► Include your personal and family goals. Define how you see your life when you reach retirement age.

► How will you balance your business and personal life? What compromises are you willing and not willing to make?

► What kind of help would you want and need? In your place of business? At home?

► Invest in your *success*. Invest in *yourself*.

Invest in Your Success

Invest in Your Business

▶ Start your business with the best equipment and materials you can afford. As your business grows, add whatever equipment and supplies you need as your income allows. Today, computers, faxes, and answering machines are almost a must.

▶ Invest in attractive stationery and business cards. It's your image and your message about your business. There are many instant print stores and office supply chains that do this type of printing inexpensively. For better paper and quality, get prices from several local printers. Always do comparison-shopping. If you don't have time, ask someone to help you. They will be helping you to invest in your business and save money.

▶ Clients and customers have to be able to find you. You have to join business and networking organizations. Determine which ones bring together the types of businesspeople you most want to network with and can possibly refer business to you. Explore which ones you'll find support from. Local chambers of commerce are good for networking with both women and men in business. Local chapters of national women's organizations are excellent for support, resources, and contacts that can be of value to you as a woman business owner. Call for information, applications, and costs. Ask other business owners in your area which ones they recommend.

▶ Determine what you can afford to spend on marketing your business. Have a budget for advertising, public relations, and promotional materials. Talk to professionals for ideas and advice. Some things you can do yourself; some things you'll need to hire an expert to do; in the long run it will be more effective and less costly. Always ask for referrals when seeking to hire an advisor or consultant.

▶ In service businesses, take your clients out for lunch periodically and send them holiday cards and (if appropriate) holiday gifts. For retail customers, also send holiday cards, decorate your place of business for seasonal holidays, and offer give-aways or discounts as you can afford to.

▶ Check out barter companies in your community. It can be a good way for you to purchase business equipment and materials as well as services and, at the same time, let others know about your business.

▶ Invest time. Attend seminars or conferences where you can gain information that is pertinent and valuable to your business. Learn how to get government contracts. Spend time at organization meetings to develop business relationships. Establish relationships with women and men in the corporate world in order to have an opportunity to tap into the lucrative corporate markets.

Invest in Yourself

▶ Learn about what you don't know that will be of value to your business. Take a course about Internet commerce, time management, strategic planning, marketing, financial planning, and public speaking. Take seminars offered by your industry group to stay up-to-date on trends and more.

▶ Attend professional conferences.

▶ Be sure you have the right clothes and image for your business. If you travel a lot, be aware of what will work for you in different places. I do not wear the same type of clothes for business meetings in Israel as I do in New York City. Honest, making a good impression counts.

▶ Invest money in taking care of *you*: body, mind, and spirit.

Sell Yourself and Get Connected

Networking and Strategic Alliances

▶ Once you've joined the right business organizations, it's important to create important strategic alliances. All successful people do. Exchange business referrals, resources, contacts, and connections. Be connected with other successful, influential people.

▶ Consider these relationships as relationship marketing. They could open doors for you to be on corporate boards where you can develop valuable strategic alliances.

▶ Network with clear, up-front goals. Networking is about more than shaking hands and giving out business cards—although be sure you always have plenty of business cards with you. Make follow-up calls. Send follow-up notes. Stay in touch with good contacts you make. This is about *business*, not about being *loved*. Stop being concerned people will think you want something from them. You do! They also want something from you. It's called *business*.

▶ Make a positive impression. Please offer a firm handshake. Don't shake hands like a wet fish!

▶ Listen well. Pay attention. Be responsive. Be aware of your body language. Don't look bored, even if you are!

▶ Volunteer with at least one or two community service organizations. Select ones that fit an interest or a passion you might have. It's a great way to connect with people, become known, and feel good about what you're giving back to your community. The good word gets around about you and what you're doing. It's the best public relations for you and your business.

▶ Serve on boards of these volunteer organizations. If you're a valued and active member, these organizations will want to consider you for their boards, providing you with a presence and stature that brings excellent credibility to you and your business. Business success used to be location, location, location. Today, business success is often defined and accomplished by *who you know, who you know, who you know ... and who knows you!*

▶ Don't be shy about promoting yourself and your business.

MY STORY

What Is Success Really About?

My favorite question when someone tells me they have a Road-Block or MindBlock is "What is it really about?"

My rabbi friend said I ask Socratic questions so I can reach into the heart of the issue. I ask these questions regarding business to uncover the secrets that keep us from facing the real issues that interfere with being a success in business.

There have been times I've had to ask myself, "What is this really about? What is success to me? What will really satisfy my hunger that has driven me throughout my adult life?"

I've experienced the ups and downs of being an entrepreneur. I started several businesses. I've had wonderful success and some not so wonderful. I'm never willing to give up and I maintain a determination and tunnel vision to keep me focused.

My success, in part, is my accomplishment of never giving up my determination and belief. Even though I've had a great deal of business and financial success, I've wanted to be a published author ever since I was a teenager. I promised myself I would do what I had to do to make it happen. It's what I needed to do to satisfy a personal hunger.

Where does a person's determination and belief come from? We need people to love and care about us and for us to care about them. We need to believe in ourselves, have courage, and trust our abilities and strengths. Often we need that "added value" of someone believing so much in us that we are encouraged and motivated by their actions. Our voices are heard and our talents are seen. My family and close friends have been my "added value."

I've written this book and, in the process, I've given myself my dream. It makes me smile. I plan to write more.

Now all I need is a month somewhere beautiful, perhaps even romantic, in the sun!

PARTING WORD

A woman's success is definitely not a four-letter word.

THE WOMAN'S BUSINESS THERAPIST'S 12 REMINDERS FOR WOMEN ENTREPRENEURS FOR ELIMINATING MINDBLOCKS AND ROADBLOCKS TO SUCCESS

A dozen reminders to let you know someone really understands what it takes for you to be a woman in business, that you're not alone, and that you deserve success:

1. Know what your own MindBlocks and RoadBlocks are.

2. Be willing to move beyond your personal history and choose the life you want and deserve.

3. Be clear about what you really want to have and do.

4. Question the values and roles you were taught and inherited.

5. Listen to your own voice and instincts.

6. Share concerns and ideas with people whose ideas and values you trust. Vent to a good friend when necessary.

7. Get help. Get good help. Be connected to good and supportive people.

8. Pay attention. Be accountable and responsible.

9. Network. Create strategic alliances. Develop strong supportive business relationships.

10. Find the best way for you to deal effectively and comfortably with men in business.

11. Maintain a balance between your business and personal life.

12. Have high expectations. You're entitled.

Parting Word

Action and faith are great partners for success.

RESOURCES FOR WOMEN BUSINESS OWNERS

ORGANIZATIONAL RESOURCES

The Woman's Business Therapist
E-mail: marciar101@aol.com
Web: www.womanbusinesstherapist.com

Alliance of Business Women International
P.O. Box 2904
Corrales, NM 87048
800-606-2294, 505-890-1704
Phone: 800-606-2294
Fax: 505-890-1701
E-mail: abwiexe@aol.com
Web: www.abwi.org

American Woman's Economic Development Corp.
216 E. 45th Street, 10th Floor
New York, NY 10017
Phone: 212-692-9100
Fax: 212-692-9296
Web: orgs.women.connect.com/awed

Business and Professional Women/USA
2012 Massachusetts Avenue, NW
Washington, DC 20036
Phone: 202-293-1100
Fax: 202-861-0298
Web: www.bpwusa.org

Business Women Leadership Foundation
1700 K Street NW, Suite 1005
Washington, DC 20006
Phone: 202-822-5010
Fax: 202-293-1508

Business Women's Network
1146 19th Street NW, Third Floor
Washington, DC 20036
Phone: 202-466-8212
Fax: 202-833-1808
E-mail: bwn@tpag.com
Web: www.bwni.com

Center for Women's Global Leadership
Douglass College
Rutgers, The State University of New Jersey
160 Ryders Lane
New Brunswick, NJ 08901-8555
Phone: 723-932-8782
Fax: 732-932-1180
E-mail: cwgl@igc.org

Executive Women International
515 South 700 East, Suite 2F
Salt Lake City, UT 84102
Phone: 888-EWI-1229, 801-355-2800
Fax: 801-355-2852
E-mail: ewi@executivewomen.org
Web: www.executivewomen.org

Federation of Organizations for Professional Women
1825 I Street NW, Suite 400
Washington, DC 20006
Phone: 202-328-1415

Ms. Foundation for Women
120 Wall Street, 33rd Floor
New York, NY 10005
Phone: 212-742-2300
Fax: 212-742-1653
E-mail: info@ms.foundation.org
Web: www.ms.foundation.org

National Association for Female Executives, Inc.
135 W. 50th Street, 16th Floor
New York, NY 10020
Phone: 800-634-NAFE, 212-445-6235
Fax: 212-445-6228
E-mail: nafe@nafe.org
Web: www.nafe.com

National Association of Women Business Owners
1100 Wayne Avenue, Suite 830
Silver Spring, MD 20910
(NAWBO Information Service Line)
800-55-NAWBO (800-556-2926)
Phone: 301-608-2590
Fax: 301-608-2596
E-mail: national@nawbo.org

National Business Association
5151 Beltline Road, Suite 1150
Dallas, TX 75240
Phone: 800-456-0440 or 214-991-5381
Fax: 972-960-9149
E-mail: nba12@airmail.net
Web: www.nationalbusiness.org

National Chamber of Commerce for Women
10 Waterside Place, Suite 6H

New York, NY 10010
Phone: 212-685-3454

National Council of Jewish Women
National Office
53 W. 23rd Street, 6th Floor
New York, NY 10010
Phone: 212-645-4048
Fax: 212-645-7466
E-mail: mail@ncjw.org
Web: www.ncjw.org

National Foundation for Women Business Owners
1100 Wayne Avenue, Suite 830
Silver Spring, MD 20910-5603
Phone: 301-495-4975
Fax: 301-495-4979
E-mail: NFWBO@worldnet.att.net
Web: www.nfwbo.org

National Organization for Women
National Headquarters
733 15th Street NW, 2nd Floor
Washington, DC 20005
Phone: 202-628-8669
Fax: 202-785-8576
E-mail: now@now.org
Web: www.now.org

Office of Women's Business Ownership
Small Business Administration
409 Third Street SW
Washington, DC 20416
Phone: 202-205-6673
Fax: 202-205-7287

E-mail: owbo@sba.gov
Web: www.sba.gov/womeninbusiness

Organization of Women in International Trade

P.O. Box 81148
Chicago, IL 60681-0148
Phone: 312-641-1466
Fax: 414-697-2252
Web: www.owit.org

wbusiness

The Cain Group, LLC and wbusiness
265 Sunrise Highway, 2nd Floor
Rockville Centre, NY 11570
Phone: 888-333-0393 or 516-594-4900
Fax: 516-594-4569
E-mail: info@wbusiness.net
Web: www.wbusiness.net

Women's Business Development Center

Small Business Resource Center
49 NW 5th Street Suite 104
Miami, FL 33128
Phone: 305-358-8589
Fax: 305-358-7588

Women's Business Enterprise

National Council
1710 H Street NW, 7th Floor
Washington, DC 20006
Phone: 202-872-5515
Fax: 202-872-5505
E-mail: WBECERT@aol.com
Web: orgs.womenconnect.com/wbenc

Women Incorporated

333 South Grand Avenue, Suite 2450
Los Angeles, CA 90071
Phone: 800-930-3993 or 213-680-3375
Fax: 213-680-3475
Web: www.womeninc.com

Women on the Fast Track

585 Stewart Avenue, Suite 790
Garden City, NY 11530
Phone: 516-594-2367
Fax: 516-228-9488
E-mail: lucyrosen@aol.org
Web: www.womenonthefasttrack.com

Women Presidents' Organization

335 Madison, 4th Floor
New York, NY 10017
Phone: 212-818-9424
Fax: 212-818-9423
E-mail: wpo1999@aol.com
Web: womeninc.com/wpo/wpo.htm

WEB SITES

The sites listed here have lots of useful information for women entrepreneurs and business owners. Many of them include additional links to other sites. These sites will give you information, help, encouragement, and people you can ask questions of and network with.

Advancing Women
www.advancingwomen.com

American Home Business Association
www.homebusiness.com

Biz Resource Site
www.bizresource.com

Business For Women
www.businessforwomen.com

Business Resources for Women
www.womensbizresources.com

Business Women's Network Interactive
www.bwni.com

Cybergrrl, Inc.
www.cybergrrl.com

Digital-Women.com
www.digital-women.com/

Electra—Real Women, Real Life
www.electra.com

Entrepreneur Network for Women
www.network4women.com

Every Woman's Business
www.first-ladies.org/

Financial Women International
www.fwi.org

Forum for Women Entrepreneurs
www.fwe.org

Her Business
netcenter.women.com/smallbusiness/

ivillage.com—The Women's Network
www.ivillage.com

National Association for Female Executives Inc.
www.nafe.com

National Women Business Owners Corporation
www.wboc.org

Online Women's Business Center
www.onlinewbc.org

Oxygen
www.oxygen.com

WebmistressAtWork-News (E-Zine)
womeninbusiness.webmistressatwork.com/

WomaNet
www.womenbusiness.com/womanet.htm

Woman's Advantage
www.womansadvantage.com/bwa/

Woman Owned Workplaces
www.womanowned.com

Womenbiz Network
www.womenbiz.net

Women.com
www.women.com

womenCONNECT.com
www.womenconnect.com

Women in Business Cyberspace Field of Dreams
www.fodreams.com/home.html

Women'sBlvd
www.womensblvd.com

Women's Enterprise
www.womens-enterprise.com

The Women's Internet Business Directory
www.bizgrowth.com/bizdirectory.html

Women's Wire
www.womenswire.com

Womens Work
wwork.com/

Working Woman
www.workingwomanmag.com

The World Association of Women Entrepreneurs (FCEM)
www.fcem.org

WOWFactor—Women on the Web
www.wowfactor.com

NATIONAL SMALL BUSINESS DEVELOPMENT CENTERS

Alabama

Mr. John Sandefur, State Director
Alabama SBD Consortium
University of Alabama at Birmingham
2800 Milan Court, Suite 124
Birmingham, AL 35211-6908
Phone: 205-943-6750
Fax: 205-943-6752
E-mail: sandefur@uab.edu
Web: www.asbdc.org

Alaska

Ms. Jan Fredericks, State Director
Alaska SBDC
University of Alaska Anchorage
430 West Seventh Avenue, Suite 110
Anchorage, AK 99501
Phone: 907-274-7232
Fax: 907-274-9524
E-mail: anja@uaa.alaska.edu
Web: www.aksbdc.org

Arizona

Michael York, State Director
Arizona SBDC Network
2411 West 14th Street, Suite 132
Tempe, AZ 85281
Phone: 602-731-8720
Fax: 602-731-8729
E-mail: york@maricopa.edu
Web: www.dist.maricopa.edu/sbdc

Arkansas

Ms. Janet Nye, State Director
Arkansas SBDC
University of Arkansas at Little Rock
100 South Main, Suite 401
Little Rock, AR 72201
Phone: 501-324-9043
Fax: 501-324-9049
E-mail: jmnye@ualr.edu
Web: asbdc.ual.edu

California

Ms. Kimberly A. Neri, State Director
California SBDC Program
Trade & Commerce Agency
801 K Street, Suite 1700
Sacramento, CA 95814
Phone: 916-324-5068
Fax: 916-322-5084
E-mail: kneri@commerce.ca.gov
Web: commerce.ca.gov/business/small/starting /sb_sbcdcl.html

Colorado

Ms. Mary Madison, State Director
Colorado SBDC
Colorado Office of Business Development
1625 Broadway, Suite 1710
Denver, CO 80202
Phone: 303-892-3809
Fax: 303-892-3848
E-mail: Mary.Madison@state.co.us
Web: www.state.co.us/gov_dir/oed/sbdc.html

Connecticut

Mr. Dennis Gruell, State Director
Connecticut SBDC
University of Connecticut

2 Bourn Place, U-94
Storrs, CT 06269-5094
Phone: 860-486-4135
Fax: 860-486-1576
E-mail: CSBDCinformation@sba.uconn.edu
Web: www.sbdc.uconn.edu

Delaware
Mr. Clinton Tymes, State Director
Delaware SBDC
102 MBNA America Hall
Newark, DE 19716
Phone: 302-831-1555
Fax: 302-831-1423
E-mail: sbdc-info@udel.edu
Web: www.delawaresbdc.org

District of Columbia
Ms. Vicki Johnson, State Director
District of Columbia SBDC
Howard University
2600 6th Street NW, Room 128
Washington, DC 20059
Phone: 202-806-1550
Fax: 202-806-1777
E-mail: vrjohnson@howard.edu
Web: apocalypse.cldc.howard.edu/~husbdc/

Florida
Mr. Jerry G. Cartwright, State Director
Florida SBDC
University of West Florida
19 West Garden Street, Suite 302
Pensacola, FL 32501
Phone: 850-595-6060
Fax: 850-595-6070

E-mail: fsbdc@uwf.edu
Web: www.floridasbdc.com

Georgia

Mr. Henry H. Logan, State Director
Georgia SBDC
University of Georgia
Chicopee Complex
1180 East Broad Street
Athens, GA 30602-5412
Phone: 706-542-6762
Fax: 706-542-6776
E-mail: sbdcdir@uga.cc.uga.edu
Web: www.sbdc.uga.edu

Hawaii

Mr. Darryl Mleynek, State Director
Hawaii SBDC
University of Hawaii at Hilo
200 West Kawili Street
Hilo, HI 96720-4091
Phone: 808-974-7515
Fax: 808-974-7683
E-mail: darrylm@interpac.net
Web: www.hawaii-sbdc.org

Idaho

Mr. James Hogge, State Director
Idaho SBDC
Boise State University
1910 University Drive
Boise, ID 83725
Phone: 208-426-1640
Fax: 208-426-3877
E-mail: jhogge@boisestate.edu
Web: www.boisestate.edu/isbdc

Illinois

Mr. Mark Petrelli, State Director
Illinois SBDC
Dept. of Commerce & Community Affairs
620 East Adams Street, 3rd Floor
Springfield, IL 62701
Phone: 217-524-5856
Fax: 217-524-0171
E-mail: mpetrell@commerce.state.il.us
Web: www.commerce.state.il.us

Indiana

Ms. Debbie Bishop, Executive Director
Indiana SBDC
Indiana Chamber of Commerce
One North Capitol, Suite 1275
Indianapolis, IN 46204
Phone: 317-264-2820
Fax: 317-264-2806
E-mail: debbie@isbdcorp.org
Web: www.isbdcorp.org/sbdc/

Iowa

Mr. Ronald A. Manning, State Director
Iowa SBDC
Iowa State University
137 Lynn Avenue
Ames, IA 50014-7126
Phone: 515-292-6351
Fax: 515-292-0020
E-mail: rmanning@iastate.edu
Web: www.iowasbdc.org

Kansas

Ms. Brenda O'Gorman, State Director
Kansas SBDC
214 SW 6th Avenue, Suite 205

Topeka, KS 66603-3719
Phone: 785-296-6514
Fax: 785-291-3261
E-mail: ksbdc@cjnetworks.com

Kentucky
Ms. Becky Naugle, State Director
Kentucky SBDC
University of Kentucky
Center for Entrepreneurship
225 Gatton Business & Economics Building
Lexington, KY 40506-0034
Phone: 606-257-7668
Fax: 606-323-1907
E-mail: lrnaug0@pop.uky.edu
Web: www.ksbdc.org

Louisiana
Dr. John P. Baker, State Director
Louisiana SBDC
University of Louisiana at Monroe
College of Business Administration, Room 2-57
Monroe, LA 71209-6435
Phone: 318-342-5506
Fax: 318-342-5510
E-mail: brbaker@alpha.nlu.edu
Web: lsbdc.net1.nlu.edu

Maine
Mr. Charles F. Davis, State Director
Maine SBDC
University of Southern Maine
96 Falmouth Street
P.O. Box 9300
Portland, ME 04104-9300
Phone: 207-780-4420
Fax: 207-780-4810

E-mail: msbdc@usm.maine.edu
Web: www.mainesbdc.org

Maryland
Ms. Renee Sprow, State Director
Maryland SBDC
7100 Baltimore Avenue, Suite 401
College Park, MD 20740
Phone: 301-403-8300
Fax: 301-403-8303
E-mail: RSprow@mdsbdc.umd.edu
Web: www.bsos.umd.edu/sbdc

Massachusetts
Ms. Georgianna Parkin, State Director
Massachusetts SBDC
UMASS - Rm. 205
P.O. Box 34935
Amherst, MA 01001-4935
Phone: 413-545-6301
Fax: 413-545-1273
E-mail: g.parkin@umassp.edu
Web: www.umassp.edu/msbdc

Michigan
Mr. Ronald R. Hall, State Director
Michigan SBDC
Wayne State University
2727 Second Avenue, Suite 107
Detroit, MI 48201
Phone: 313-964-1798
Fax: 313-964-3648
E-mail: ron@misbdc.wayne.edu or stateoffice@misbdc.wayne.edu
Web: michigansbdc.org

Minnesota
Ms. Mary J. Kruger, State Director
Department of Trade and Economic Development

500 Metro Square
121 7th Place East
St. Paul, MN 55101-2146
Phone: 661-297-5773
Fax: 651-296-1290
E-mail: mary.kruger@state.mn.us
Web: sbe.d.umn.edu/ced/sbdc.htm

Mississippi
Mr. Walter Gurley, Jr., State Director
Mississippi SBDC
University of Mississippi
B-19 Track Drive
University, MS 38677
Phone: 662-915-5001
Fax: 662-915-5650
E-mail: msbdc@olemiss.edu
Web:www.olemiss.edu/depts/mssbdc

Missouri
Mr. Max Summers, State Director
Missouri SBDC
1205 University Avenue, Suite 300
Columbia, MO 65211
Phone: 573-882-0344
Fax: 573-884-4297
E-mail: sbdc-mso@ext.missouri.edu
Web: www.mo-sbdc.org

Montana
Mr. Ralph Kloser, State Director
Montana SBDC
Montana Department of Commerce
1424 9th Avenue
P.O. Box 200505
Helena, MT 59620
Phone: 406-444-4374

Fax: 406-444-1872
E-mail: rkloser@mt.gov
Web: commerce.mt.gov/EconDev/SBDC/SBDC.htm

Nebraska
Mr. Robert E. Bernier, State Director
Nebraska SBDC
University of Nebraska at Omaha
60th & Dodge Street, CBA Room 407
Omaha, NE 68182-0248
Phone: 402-554-2521
Fax: 402-554-3747
E-mail: rbernier@unomaha.edu
Web: nbdc.unomaha.edu

Nevada
Mr. Sam Males, State Director
Nevada SBDC
University of Nevada, Reno
College of Business Administration
Nazir Ansari Business Building-032, Room 411
Reno, NV 89557-0100
Phone: 702-784-1717
Fax: 702-784-4337
E-mail: males@unr.edu
Web: www.nsbdc.org

New Hampshire
Ms. Mary E. Collins, State Director
New Hampshire SBDC
University of New Hampshire
108 McConnell Hall
Durham, NH 03824-3593
Phone: 603-862-2200
Fax: 603-862-4876
E-mail: Mec@christa.unh.edu
Web: www.nhsbdc.org

New Jersey
Ms. Brenda Hopper,
New Jersey SBDC
Rutgers University
Graduate School of Management
49 Bleeker Street
Newark, NJ 07102
Phone: 973-353-5950
Fax: 973-353-1110
E-mail: sbdc@andromeda.rutgers.edu
Web: www.nj.com/njsbdc

New Mexico
Mr. Roy Miller, State Director
New Mexico SBDC
Santa Fe Community College
6401 Richards Avenue
Santa Fe, NM 87505
Phone: 505-428-1362
Fax: 505-428-1469
E-mail: rmiller@santa-fe.cc.nm.us
Web: www.edd.state.nm.us/SERVICES/NEWBUSINESS/sbdc.html

New York
Mr. James L. King, State Director
New York SBDC
State University of New York
State University Plaza, S-523
Albany, NY 12246
Phone: 518-443-5398
Fax: 518-465-4992
E-mail: Kingjl@sbdc.suny.edu
Web: www.nyssbdc.org

North Carolina
Mr. Scott R. Daugherty, State Director
North Carolina SBTDC

University of North Carolina
333 Fayetteville Street Mall, Suite 1150
Raleigh, NC 27601
Phone: 919-715-7272
Fax: 919-715-7777
E-mail: sdaugherty@sbtdc.org
Web: www.sbtdc.org

North Dakota
Mr. Walter Kearns, State Director
North Dakota SBDC
University of North Dakota
118 Gamble Hall, UND, Box 7308
Grand Forks, ND 58202-7308
Phone: 701-777-3700
Fax: 701-777-3225
E-mail: kearns@prairie.nodak.edu
Web: www.und.nodak.edu/dept/ndsbdc

Ohio
Ms. Holly Schick, State Director
Ohio SBDC
77 South High Street, 28th Floor
Columbus, OH 43215-6108
Phone: 614-466-2711
Fax: 614-466-0829
E-mail: hschick@odod.ohio.gov
Web: www.ohiosbdc.org

Oklahoma
Dr. Grady L. Pennington, State Director
Oklahoma SBDC
Southeastern Oklahoma State University
517 University
P.O. Box 2584, Station A
Durant, OK 74701
Phone: 800-522-6154 or 580-924-0277

Fax: 580-920-7471
E-mail: gpennington@sosu.edu
Web: www.osbdc.org

Oregon

Dr. Edward (Sandy) Cutler, State Director
Oregon SBDC
Lane Community College
44 West Broadway, Suite 501
Eugene, OR 97401-3021
Phone: 541-726-2250
Fax: 541-345-6006
E-mail: cutlers@lanecc.edu
Web: www.bizcenter.org

Pennsylvania

Gregory Higgins, State Director
Pennsylvania SBDC
The Wharton School, University of Pennsylvania
Vance Hall, 4th Floor
3733 Spruce Street
Philadelphia, PA 19104-6374
Phone: 215-898-1219
Fax: 215-573-2135
E-mail: ghiggins@wharton.upenn.edu
Web: www.pasbdc.org

Rhode Island

Mr. Robert Hamlin, State Director
Rhode Island SBDC
Bryant College
1150 Douglas Pike
Smithfield, RI 02917-1284
Phone: 401-232-6111
Fax: 401-232-6933
E-mail: rhamlin@bryant.edu or admin@RISBDC.org
Web: www.risbdc.org

South Carolina
Mr. John Lenti, State Director
The Frank L. Roddey SBDC
University of South Carolina
College of Business Administration
Hipp Building
Columbia, SC 29208
Phone: 803-777-4907
Fax: 803-777-4403
E-mail: lenti@darla.badm.scarolina.edu
Web: sbdcweb.badm.sc.edu

South Dakota
Mr. Wade Druin, State Director
South Dakota SBDC
University of South Dakota
School of Business
414 East Clark Street
Vermillion, SD 57069
Phone: 605-677-5287
Fax: 605-677-5427
E-mail: SBDC@sundance.usd.edu
Web: www.usd.edu/brbinfo/brb/sbdc

Tennessee
Dr. Kenneth J. Burns, State Director
Tennessee SBDC
University of Memphis
Bldg. 1, South Campus, Getwell Road
Memphis, TN 38152-0001
Phone: 901-678-2500
Fax: 901-678-4072
E-mail: kburns@cc.memphis.edu
Web: www.tsbdc.memphis.edu

Texas—Dallas
Ms. Liz Klimback, Regional Director

North Texas SBDC
Bill J. Priest Institute for Economic Development
1402 Corinth Street
Dallas, TX 75215
Phone: 214-860-5831
Fax: 214-860-5813
E-mail: emk9402@dcccd.edu

Texas—San Antonio
Mr. Robert M. McKinley,
Regional Director
UTSA South Texas Border SBDC
UTSA Downtown Center
1222 North Main Street, Suite 450
San Antonio, TX 78212
Phone: 210-458-2450
Fax: 210-458-2464
E-mail: rmckinley@utsa.edu

Texas—Houston
Mr. Mike Young, Executive Director
Houston SBDC
University of Houston
1100 Louisiana, Suite 500
Houston, TX 77002
Phone: 713-752-8444
Fax: 713-756-1500
E-mail: fyoung@uh.edu
Web: www.smbizsolutions.uh.edu

Texas—Lubbock
Mr. Craig Bean, State Director
N.W. Texas SBDC
Texas Tech University
2579 South Loop 289, Suite 114
Lubbock, TX 79423
Phone: 806-745-3973

Fax: 806-745-6207
E-mail: odbea@ttacs.ttu.edu

Utah
Mr. Michael C. Finnerty, State Director
Utah SBDC
1623 South State Street
Salt Lake City, UT 84115
Phone: 801-957-3480
Fax: 801-957-3489
E-mail: Finnermi@slcc.edu
Web: www.slcc.edu/utahsbdc

Vermont
Mr. Donald Kelpinski, State Director
Vermont SBDC
Vermont Technical College
Maine Street
P.O. Box 422
Randolph Center, VT 05061
Phone: 802-728-9101
Fax: 802-728-3026
E-mail: dkelpins@vtc.vsc.edu
Web: www.vtsbdc.org

Virginia
Mr. Robert Wilburn, State Director
Virginia SBDC
Department of Business Assistance
707 E. Main Street, Suite 300
P.O. Box 446
Richmond, VA 23219
Phone: 804-371-8253
Fax: 804-225-3384
E-mail: rwilburn@dba.state.va.us
Web: www.dba.state.va.us/SBDMain.htm

Washington
Ms. Carolyn Clark, State Director
Washington SBDC
Washington State University
501 Johnson Tower
P.O. Box 644851
Pullman, WA 99164-4851
Phone: 509-335-1576
Fax: 509-335-0949
E-mail: clrk@wsu.edu

West Virginia
Dr. Hazel Kroesser Palmer, State Director
West Virginia SBDC
950 Kanawha Boulevard East, Suite 200
Charleston, WV 25301
Phone: 304-558-2960
Fax: 304-558-0127
E-mail: palmeh@mail.wvnet.edu
Web: www.wvsbdc.org

Wisconsin
Ms. Erica Kauten, State Director
Wisconsin SBDC
University of Wisconsin
432 North Lake Street, Room 423
Madison, WI 53706
Phone: 608-263-7794
Fax: 608-263-7830
E-mail: sbdc@uwex.edu
Web: www.uwex.edu/sbdc

Wyoming
Ms. Diane Wolverton, State Director
WSBDC/State Network Office
University of Wyoming
Wyoming Hall, Room 414

P.O. Box 3922
Laramie, WY 82071-3922
Phone: 307-766-3505
Fax: 307-766-3406
E-mail: DDW@uwyo.edu
Web: www.uwyo.edu/sbdc

Pacific Islands
Mr. Jack Peters, Director
Pacific Islands SBDC Network
College of Business and Public Administration
303 University Drive, UOG Station
Mangilao, GU 96923
Phone: 671-735-2590
Fax: 671-734-2002
E-mail: jackp@uog.edu
Web: www.uog.edu/sbdc

Puerto Rico
Ms. Carmen Marti, State Director
Puerto Rico SBDC
Inter American University of Puerto Rico
Edificio Union Plaza, #701
416 Ponce de León Avenue
Hato Rey, PR 00918
Phone: 787-763-6811
Fax: 787-763-6875
E-mail: cmarti@ns.inter.edu
Web: www.prsbdc.org

Virgin Islands
Mr. Reginald Ian Hodge, State Director
UVI SBDC
8000 Nisky Center, Suite 202
St. Thomas, VI 00802-5804
Phone: 340-776-3206
Fax: 340-775-3756
E-mail: ihodge@uvi.edu